D0025915

STUDY SKILLS FOR ACADEMIC WRITING

STUDENT'S BOOK

Other titles in the English for Academic Study series:

WHITE, R. and MCGOVERN, D.
Writing

MCGOVERN, D., MATTHEWS, M. and MACKAY, S.
Reading

The English for Academic Purposes series:

ST JOHN YATES, C.
Agriculture

VAUGHAN JAMES, C.
Business Studies

WALKER, T.
Computer Studies

ST JOHN YATES, C.
Earth Sciences

ST JOHN YATES, C.
Economics

JOHNSON, D. and JOHNSON, C. M.
General Engineering

JAMES, D. V.
Medicine

ENGLISH FOR ACADEMIC STUDY SERIES

STUDY SKILLS FOR ACADEMIC WRITING

Student's Book

John Trzeciak
and S. E. Mackay

PHOENIX
ELT

PRENTICE HALL MACMILLAN

New York   London   Toronto   Sydney   Tokyo   Singapore

Published 1995 by
Phoenix ELT
Campus 400, Spring Way
Maylands Avenue, Hemel Hempstead
Hertfordshire, HP2 7EZ
A division of Prentice Hall International

First published 1994 by Prentice Hall International

© International Book Distributors Ltd, 1994

All rights reserved. No reproduction, copy or transmission
of this publication may be made without written permission
or in accordance with the provisions of the Copyright, Designs
and Patents Act 1988, or under the terms of any licence
permitting limited copying issued by the Copyright Licensing
Agency, 90 Tottenham Court Road, London, W1P 9HE.

Typeset in 11/12 Garamond
by Fakenham Photosetting Limited

Printed and bound in Great Britain by
Redwood Books, Trowbridge, Wiltshire

Library of Congress Cataloging in Publication Data

Trzeciak, John.
    Study skills for academic writing. Student's book / John Trzeciak
and S.E. MacKay.
        p.   cm. – (English for academic study)
    ISBN 0-13-017856-X
    1. English language – Textbooks for foreign speakers.   2. English
language – Rhetoric – Problems, exercises, etc.   3. Study, Method of –
Problems, exercises, etc.   4. Report writing – Problems, exercises,
etc.   I. Mackay, Susan E.   II. Title.   III. Series.
PE1128.T73   1994
808'.042 – dc20   94-19763
                                                                        CIP

British Library Cataloguing in Publication Data

A catalogue record for this book is available from the British Library

ISBN 0–13–017856–X

    3   4   5   98   97   96

CONTENTS

DEDICATION

This book is dedicated to the memory of Don McGovern (1949–1993), writer and poet, whose imagination, care and profundity in wide-ranging concerns of language and the performing arts won him respect wherever he worked.

His work on the Reading and Writing volumes in this series was completed shortly before his untimely death.

ACKNOWLEDGEMENTS

Thanks are due to the many teachers who have made valuable comments on their use of this material on the Pre-sessional English Language course run by the Centre for Applied Language Studies at Reading University; especially to Irwin Buchanan, Rosemary Dorey, David Field, Kate Gaze, Irene Guy, John Lake, Deborah Sayer and John Slaght.

Thanks are also due to the following for helpful comments on different parts of the material: George Blue of Southampton University who reviewed an early version of the first unit; Sue Price of Reading University Library who provided invaluable help with Unit 4 during various stages of its development; and the following staff at CALS: Mark Rignall, particularly for his help with organisation of the material and for coming up with three texts that were difficult to find for Unit 3, Don McGovern, who offered suggestions on several revised tasks, Pat Bennett, who helped with copyright correspondence and typed early drafts of many of the tasks, Clare Furneaux, Pauline Robinson, Alan Tonkyn and Cyril Weir.

The authors and publishers wish to acknowledge the following use of material:

Blackwell Publishers for the pages from *The ELT Curriculum* by Ronald V. White; the quotation from J. Short 'Cities as if only capital matters' in *The Humane City*; and the extracts from 'Politics and the State' by Andrew Mason in *Political Studies* and *An Introduction to Sociolinguistics* by Ronald Wardhaugh.
TESOL Quartely for 'What unskilled ESL students do as they write: a classroom study of composing' by Ann Raimes.
Scott Mainwaring and *Comparative Politics* for 'Politicians, parties and electoral systems: Brazil in comparative perspective'.
P. C. Robinson for the prelim page of *Living English*.
Quarto Publishing plc, published in the UK by Tiger Books International plc, for *The Encyclopedia of Practical Photography* by M. Freeman.
The Times Higher Educational Supplement for 'Salaries rise in line with fees' (15.3.91); 'Politics of music take centre stage' (12.4.91); and 'Japan paves way for big foreign influx' (15.3.91); John Greenlees for the last-mentioned of these articles.
Finance and Development for the extracts from 'Bicycles, rickshaws, and carts in Asian cities'; 'Managing the world's forests' by Narendra Sharma and Raymond

Rowe; 'Industrial policies of industrial countries' by Clemens Boonekamp; 'Management of cultural property in bank projects' by Robert Goodland; 'The changing economics of steel' by Robert R. Miller; and 'Government expenditure and growth' by Jack Diamond.

The American Political Science Association and Roger Masters for 'Evolutionary biology and political theory'.

Longman Group UK Limited for the extract 'Vitamins' from *Animal Nutrition* by P. McDonald *et al.*

Oxford University Press for the extracts from *Language Two* by Heidi Dulay, Marina Burt and Stephen Krashen and *Fundamental Concepts of Language Teaching* by H. H. Stern.

National Geographic Magazine for the extract from 'Exploring a sunken realm in Australia' by H. Hauser.

IOP Publishing and Philip Bligh for the extracts from 'The implications of reductionist physics for human culpability'.

ELT Journal for the extracts from 'Theorizing from the classroom' by E. Ramani, first published in *ELT Journal* 41/1, January 1987; and 'Teacher intention and learner interpretation' by B. Kumaravadivelu, first published in *ELT Journal* 45/2, April 1991, © Oxford University Press 1987 and 1991.

International Affairs for the extract from 'International migration and regional stability' by Jonas Widgren, which first appeared in vol. 66, no. 4, 1990, and is reproduced with permission.

Catena for the extracts from 'Hydrologic and sediment responses to simulated rainfall on desert hillslopes in Southern Arizona' by A. D. Abrahams, A. J. Parsons and Shiu-hung Luk; and 'Determining the causes of pleistocene stream aggradation in the central coastal areas of Western Australia' by K. H. Wyrwoll.

The British Journal for the Philosophy of Science for the conclusion of 'Scientific realism and postmodern philosophy' by Nancy Murphy; and the extracts from 'Why scientists gather evidence' by Patrick Maher.

The Journal of the World Trade for the introduction from 'Intellectual Property, injury and international trade' by Robert M. Feinberg; and the extracts from 'An assessment of the environmental and economic implications of toxic-waste disposal in Sub-Saharan Africa' by Bernard I. Logan.

Town Planning Review for the introduction from 'Planning for Strathclyde's regeneration' by Moira Munro and Peter Symon.

The Computer Journal for the conclusion from 'Integrative deductive database system implementation: a scientific study' by D. A. Bell, J. Shao, and M. E. C. Hull.

The Institution of Environmental Health Officers for 'Noise, stress and human behaviour' by Dylan M. Jones in *Environmental Health*, August 1990.

World Animal Review (no longer publishing) for 'Genetic improvement of livestock, using nucleus breeding units' by C. Smith.

The Observer for 'The gulf between Professor Boffin and Joe Public' by Susan Young (2.2.92).

The New Scientist for 'Surveying the extent of public ignorance' by Lynda Birke (18.8.90).

The University of Reading Bulletin for the table in Unit 4.
The Central Statistical Office for the figures in Unit 4.

Special thanks are due to *The Independent* and *The Guardian* in allowing the use of articles.
The Independent for 'Not just a cosmetic idea' by M. Smith (23.1.89); 'Out of the oceans and on to faster bicycles' by John Emsley (22.4.91); 'The greatest threat on earth' by L. Timberlake (12.9.88); 'Why it is absolutely necessary to go on naming names' by J. E. Milner (1.8.88); 'A burning passion for knowledge' by Beverly Halstead (9.11.87).
The Guardian for 'Fire stones support catastrophe theory' by David Keys (November 1988); and 'The billion dollar question marks' by Damien Lewis (8.6.90).

In spite of their best efforts, the writers and publishers have been unable to trace the authors of the following extracts:

'Fire stones support catastrophe theory' by David Keys; and 'The persistent stereotype: children's images of scientists' by Janice Emens McAdam, *Physics Education*, 25, 1990.

They will be pleased to discuss rights if the authors contact them.

INTRODUCTION

AIMS

The overall aim of this book is to ensure that you feel confident in coping with the extended written work which may be assigned to you by your subject tutors during your course of study in a college or university where English is the medium of instruction.

You will be aware that different countries have different academic traditions. It may be that the tradition you have worked in before is very similar to the one you would encounter in an English-speaking environment; however, it may be that there are certain differences in specific areas and expectations. In order for you to do well in your future course of study, it is important for you to be aware of what is expected of you and to be fully acquainted with certain conventions in the academic traditions in most of the English-speaking world.

This book will concentrate on the following areas:

- surveying a book or article
- extraction and synthesis of relevant information
- summarising and/or integrating information and ideas (without plagiarism)
- producing a coherent, well-organised piece of written work
- the correct layout of work (title and contents pages, bibliography, etc.)
- developing the ability to work on your own
- developing a critical attitude towards your work
- developing evaluative reading skills.

The book has five units. The aims of each unit are set out briefly on the first page of the unit. The first section (Guide) gives information and advice that you will require in the Tasks that form the second section of the unit. Some short tasks are occasionally included in the Guide section.

Combining the knowledge and skills from your previous academic experience with the work you do in this book will enable you to utilise effectively the facilities available to you when writing an informed piece of work. It is hoped that by the time you have completed the Guide and Task sections in the first four units of the book, you will have a sufficient grasp of all the skills needed to write a long academic essay in English, which is the major task in the final unit.

Stages in an extended academic essay

Using the material in this book, you will study and practise the skills necessary at different stages of producing an *extended* piece of academic writing (e.g. an essay, a report, a dissertation). The material is intended to prepare you for the final task of writing an extended essay in your own subject area.

Look at the stages shown below. They indicate progression from the initial research stage to the finished product. You are likely to go through most of these stages when writing an extended academic essay, though not necessarily in exactly the same order as below. You can look through the book or examine the contents page to see which stages are dealt with in each of the five units.

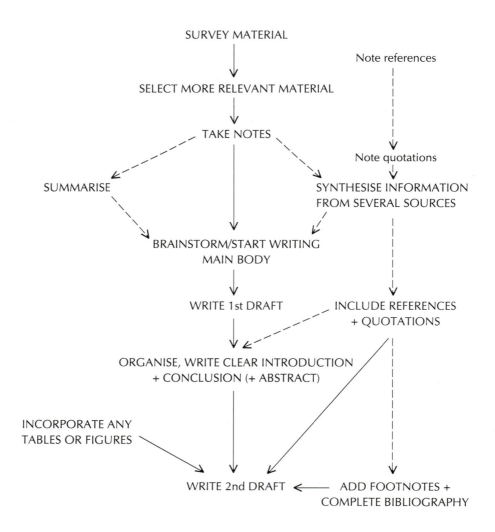

UNIT 1

SURVEYING MATERIAL

MAIN SKILLS	TASKS CORRESPONDING TO SKILLS
SURVEYING MATERIAL BY LOOKING AT:	
THE TITLE	TASK 1
THE CONTENTS PAGE	TASKS 2 + 3
THE INDEX	TASK 4
THE BLURB	TASK 5
THE FIRST AND LAST PARAGRAPH.	TASK 6
THE INTRODUCTION.	TASK 7
THE PRINTING HISTORY	TASK 8

AIMS

In this unit, you will practise finding out about the content of a book (or journal article) mainly from reading information that is *outside the main body* of the text. By looking at items such as the title, contents page or blurb, you may be able to discover whether the main body deals with what is of interest to you for your work.

SURVEYING A BOOK

When you are looking for suitable material for your written work, you will often have to assess the value of books you are unacquainted with. Surveying a book is extremely useful if you are working in a new subject area, if you do not know what is available in the subject area or if you do not know the works of a particular author. The ability to assess materials will also save a lot of time as you will be able to discard quickly any irrelevant or outdated material.

3

You may wish to find information on a particular topic you are interested in or have been given for an assignment. If you have been given adequate references, you can consult these immediately for suitable information. However, it may be that you are uncertain what line of investigation to follow or what materials may be available on a particular subject. In that case, you should consult a library catalogue if you have access to one.

Having discovered a book which may be suitable, you will need to inspect it more closely to see whether it will be of value. When searching for relevant information, you will not necessarily have to read the whole of the book. Possibly only one section of a chapter will be useful.

To discover the possible usefulness of a book, a quick inspection of the following will help you:

- acknowledgements (an author's or publisher's statement expressing thanks for help in the preparation of a book and for the use of the works of other authors)
- book title and title page (these give the sub-title if there is one)
- contents page (the main contents will be given in Arabic numerals)
- foreword (introductory remarks, usually by someone who knows the author's work)
- preface (an introductory section explaining how and why a book was written – page numbers are given in Roman numerals)
- printing history (i.e. date of publication, edition, reprints etc.)
- index (an alphabetical list of people, subjects etc. mentioned in the text of the book – usually to be found at the back of a book)
- appendix (supplementary section to the main text of the book containing additional information)
- selected chapters (first and last paragraphs)
- bibliography
- blurb (the publisher's description of the book).

See examples of these items at the end of this Unit 1 Guide section.

When surveying a book, always note the date of its publication. The date is important as it gives an indication of how up-to-date the contents are. If you are looking for the latest ideas and the publication date seems old, check to see if there is a later edition.

There are recognised authorities in most subject areas. If the author of a book is unknown to you, you should find out all you can about him or her. The preface, foreword or blurb are sections of a book that may give you some useful information. They can tell you about the author, the author's concerns in writing the book and any approaches or theories supported by the author. The bibliography will indicate the authorities and range of works consulted by the author. It will also provide you with further sources of information for you to follow up.

TITLE

What does the title suggest to you? Most titles of academic books and articles give factual information and can be understood easily by the specialist, so in many instances it should be possible to find out from a title whether an article or book is relevant to your needs. Occasionally, however, the language of the title may be figurative and therefore potentially misleading. You will notice such titles in a few of the articles, or extracts from articles, in this book. They are much more common in newspaper articles but can also be found in academic journals and books.

Short task

Look at the following examples of titles of articles which you may come across in this book. Which of these enable you to reliably predict the content of the articles they head?

1. Noise, stress and human behaviour
2. The billion dollar question marks
3. Industrial policies of industrial countries
4. Out of the oceans and on to faster bicycles
5. The persistent stereotype: children's images of scientists

---

CONTENTS PAGE, PREFACE, FIRST AND LAST PARAGRAPHS

The contents page will give you more detailed information on the contents of a book. Often a book is divided into sections, units or chapters which are then subdivided. The main headings will help you select possible useful sections.

When you need to look for specific information in a book, you may use the contents and index pages (see next section) to help you. If there is no mention of the information you are looking for, you may then look quickly through the text for mention of particular words or phrases related to your topic.

A more detailed description of the contents of a book with an explanation of why and how it came to be written will be found in an introduction or preface. Similarly, most longer academic articles will be preceded by an introduction, clearly set apart and labelled. Articles, dissertations and theses may also be preceded by a brief account of their content, known as an *abstract*.

Looking at the first and last paragraphs may also be a useful way of finding out about the content of a chapter in a book or a short article. This may avoid wasting time reading irrelevant material.

Index

The index (at the back of a book) gives you an alphabetical list of topics that are covered in the book. The contents page may not mention directly the topic you are interested in, whereas the index may. The index should also indicate the pages covering the topic. However, even though a topic may be mentioned several times, this does not mean that it is dealt with in great detail in a book.

Printing history (imprint page)

This can normally be found on one of the first pages (called the prelims). In the case of an old book, it is worth checking to see whether this is the first publication of the book and whether anything has been done to bring it more up to date since then. If there has been more than one edition, this will help you assess the popularity of the book and thus its usefulness as a core text. Librarians can help you to trace earlier or later editions, according to your needs.

Blurb

The blurb (i.e. the publisher's comments) will be found on the jacket of the book. Not only should it give you a description of the contents, and possibly some information about the author, but you may also discover what kind of reader the book was written for, and whether the author is experienced in knowing the needs of the reader. This will help you assess whether the book is written at an appropriate level for you.

Examples

On the following pages you will find examples of:

- a title page
- a contents page
- an index
- a blurb
- a printing history
- a list of books in a series
- acknowledgements
- a note to the reader.

The items above are all taken from the same book.

1. TITLE PAGE

THE ELT CURRICULUM — (a)

Design, Innovation and Management — (b)

Ronald V. White — (c)

Basil Blackwell

(d)

2. CONTENTS PAGE

Contents

3. INDEX

Index

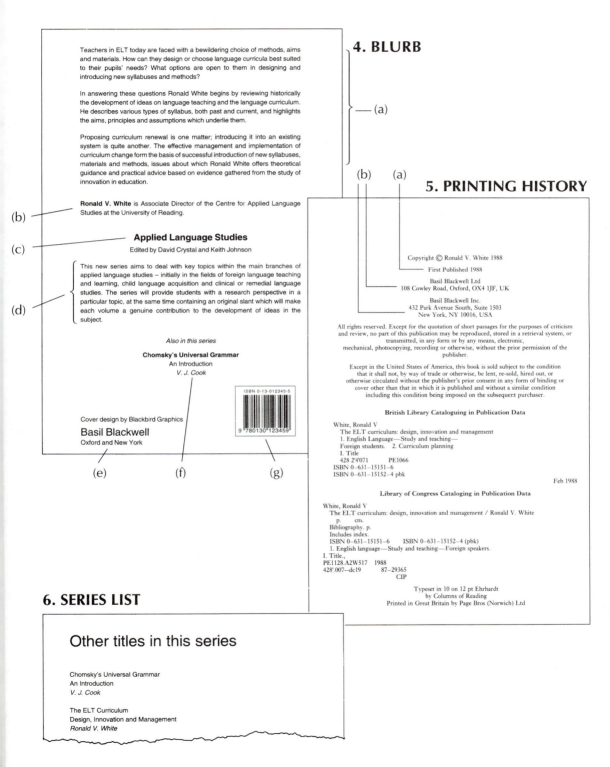

4. BLURB

— (a)

Teachers in ELT today are faced with a bewildering choice of methods, aims and materials. How can they design or choose language curricula best suited to their pupils' needs? What options are open to them in designing and introducing new syllabuses and methods?

In answering these questions Ronald White begins by reviewing historically the development of ideas on language teaching and the language curriculum. He describes various types of syllabus, both past and current, and highlights the aims, principles and assumptions which underlie them.

Proposing curriculum renewal is one matter; introducing it into an existing system is quite another. The effective management and implementation of curriculum change form the basis of successful introduction of new syllabuses, materials and methods, issues about which Ronald White offers theoretical guidance and practical advice based on evidence gathered from the study of innovation in education.

(b) — **Ronald V. White** is Associate Director of the Centre for Applied Language Studies at the University of Reading.

(c) — **Applied Language Studies**

Edited by David Crystal and Keith Johnson

(d) This new series aims to deal with key topics within the main branches of applied language studies – initially in the fields of foreign language teaching and learning, child language acquisition and clinical or remedial language studies. The series will provide students with a research perspective in a particular topic, at the same time containing an original slant which will make each volume a genuine contribution to the development of ideas in the subject.

Also in this series

Chomsky's Universal Grammar
An Introduction
V. J. Cook

ISBN 0-13-012345-5

Cover design by Blackbird Graphics

Basil Blackwell
Oxford and New York

9 780130 123459

(e)   (f)   (g)

5. PRINTING HISTORY

(b)   (a)

Copyright © Ronald V. White 1988

First Published 1988

Basil Blackwell Ltd
108 Cowley Road, Oxford, OX4 1JF, UK

Basil Blackwell Inc.
432 Park Avenue South, Suite 1503
New York, NY 10016, USA

All rights reserved. Except for the quotation of short passages for the purposes of criticism and review, no part of this publication may be reproduced, stored in a retrieval system, or transmitted, in any form or by any means, electronic, mechanical, photocopying, recording or otherwise, without the prior permission of the publisher.

Except in the United States of America, this book is sold subject to the condition that it shall not, by way of trade or otherwise, be lent, re-sold, hired out, or otherwise circulated without the publisher's prior consent in any form of binding or cover other than that in which it is published and without a similar condition including this condition being imposed on the subsequent purchaser.

British Library Cataloguing in Publication Data

White, Ronald V
  The ELT curriculum: design, innovation and management
  1. English Language—Study and teaching—
  Foreign students.   2. Curriculum planning
  I. Title
  428 2'4'071   PE1066
  ISBN 0–631–15151–6
  ISBN 0–631–15152–4 pbk

Feb 1988

Library of Congress Cataloging in Publication Data

White, Ronald V
  The ELT curriculum: design, innovation and management / Ronald V. White
    p.   cm.
  Bibliography. p.
  Includes index.
  ISBN 0–631–15151–6   ISBN 0–631–15152–4 (pbk)
  1. English language—Study and teaching—Foreign speakers.
  I. Title.,
  PE1128.A2W517   1988
  428'.007--dc19   87–29365
                   CIP

Typeset in 10 on 12 pt Ehrhardt
by Columns of Reading
Printed in Great Britain by Page Bros (Norwich) Ltd

6. SERIES LIST

Other titles in this series

Chomsky's Universal Grammar
An Introduction
V. J. Cook

The ELT Curriculum
Design, Innovation and Management
Ronald V. White

7. ACKNOWLEDGEMENTS

Acknowledgements

Authors always take a great risk: they receive praise if their work is good – and criticism if it isn't. Whatever the reception of this publication, I should like to distribute some praise of my own. Firstly, to the students who have attended the courses which provided the basis for this book. Secondly, to my colleagues, for their helpful suggestions. Thirdly, to Keith Johnson, series editor, for his critical comments and encouragement. Fourthly, to Sue Vice, for her keen editorial eye which identified many a solecism before it reached print. Finally, but most significantly, to my wife, Nora, for the kind of support and understanding which only she can provide.

The blame for what follows is entirely mine.

The author and the publishers are grateful to the following for permission to reproduce material which originally appeared elsewhere: The Council for Educational Technology for the United Kingdom, for two figures from R. Havelock (1971) 'The utilization of educational research and development', *British Journal of Educational Technology*, 1, 2/2: 84–97. The British Council for figures from *Dunford House Seminar 1979: ELT Course Design*; *ELT Documents 116, Language Teaching Projects for the Third World*; *ELT Documents 118, General English Syllabus Design*, copyright © The British Council. B. T. Batsford Ltd for a figure from R. T. Bell (1981) *An Introduction to Applied Linguistics: Approaches and Methods in Language Teaching*. Unesco for a figure from A. M. Huberman (1973) *Understanding Change in Education: An Introduction* copyright © Unesco 1973. Cambridge University Press for figures, one from J. Yalden (1983) *The Communicative Syllabus: Evolution, Design and Implementation*; and one from J. C. Richards and T. Rodgers (1986) *Approach and Methods in Language Teaching*. Simon and Schuster for a figure from C. Candlin and D. Murphy (eds) (1987) *Lancaster Practical Papers in ELT*, vol. 7.

Ron White
Reading

8. NOTE TO THE READER

Note to the reader

This book is arranged in four parts, of which each contains a number of chapters. Each chapter has a number of sections and the final two include a summary of the chapter and suggested follow-up reading.

In the Appendix, there are follow-up activities for each chapter. These activities are intended to be done by groups, and they should involve discussion. Some of the activities can also be done individually; they are linked to the content of each chapter, and provide some 'hands on' or practical development of the points covered in the chapters themselves.

You may find it useful to skim the follow-up activities *before* you read each chapter.

Key and notes to examples shown

1. *Title page*
   (a) title
   (b) sub-title
   (c) author
   (d) publisher

2. *Contents page*

   The introductory pages of the book (prelims) are indicated in Roman numerals such as (vii); the main section in ordinary Arabic numerals such as 7. In the example, the prelim sections consist of 'Printing history', 'Series list', 'Note to the reader', 'Acknowledgements' and 'Contents'. There is no preface or foreword in this book. Later editions might carry one.

3. *Index*

   Compare the kind of information given in the index with that of the contents page. Whereas the contents page gives the main sections of the book and the titles of chapters, the index refers to topics/sub-topics, authors etc. (e.g. Alexander) contained within the body of the work.

4. *Blurb*

   This is usually to be found on the back cover or jacket of a book. It will probably contain:
   (a) a publisher's description
   (b) brief details about the author
   (c) the book series to which this book belongs
   (d) a description of the series.

   In addition, the back cover or jacket may give details such as the ones shown in the example:
   (e) other titles in the series
   (f) the publisher
   (g) the international standard book number (ISBN) (this is useful if you wish to order the book through a bookseller).

5. *Printing history*
   (a) the date of publication
   (b) the name and address of the publisher.

6. *Series list*

   This book is one of a new series. Here we are given the titles of the other books in the series.

7. *Acknowledgements*

   The author's expression of thanks for help in the preparation of the book.

8. *Note to the reader*

   Extra useful information for the reader has been included.

UNIT 1

SURVEYING MATERIAL: TASKS

TASK 1

Below there are nine titles taken from books and journal articles. Choose four of the titles and for each one think of a few questions to which the text might supply answers. Subject areas are given in brackets.

(a) Agriculture in semi-arid environments (Agriculture)

(b) Extending the shelf-life of ready meals (Food Microbiology)

(c) Influences and constraints on curriculum development in the Third World (Science Education)

(d) Economics of change in less-developed countries (Economics)

(e) A critique of the Ruling Elite Model (Political Science)

(f) The physiology of meditation and mystical states of consciousness (Physiology)

(g) Some factors affecting the spatial distribution of land values in the capital cities of three industrialised countries (Urban Geography)

(h) The theory of imagination in Classical and Medieval thought (Literature)

(i) Methods of testing soils for civil engineering purposes (Soil Science)

TASK 2

Look at the contents page on the next page. Below is a list of six topics. Fit each topic to the appropriate part of the book, as in the first example.

(a) Scattered radiation   *Part 5*

(b) Radiographic screens   _____

(c) Geometric principles   _____

(d) Fundamentals of processing   _____

(e) The radiographic process   _____

(f) Factors governing exposure   _____

Task 3

You will often need to work out which chapter of a book deals with information you are looking for. Imagine you want to find information on the specific subjects listed below from the contents page that follows. Write down the number of the chapter, as in the first example.

(a) The basic principles of shadow formation on radiographs   *Chapter 2.2*

(b) Indications for the use of lead foil screens   *Chapter* _____

(c) The chemistry of automatic processing   *Chapter* _____

(d) Essential features in making a radiograph   *Chapter* _____

(e) The effect of contrast on detail in a radiograph   *Chapter* _____

(f) How masks and diagrams can reduce scatter   *Chapter* _____

Contents

Task 4

Look back at the index on page 8 and write down the page(s) you would look at for information on the following:

(a) characteristics of innovation
(b) modern language teaching and curriculum studies
(c) curriculum evaluation
(d) natural grading.

Task 5

Below are three blurbs from the covers of books. Imagine you are looking for a book on academic writing that would suit your needs. Read the blurbs and decide which one describes a book that would suit your needs best.

> 1. Academic writing is a skill that can be learned rapidly. This book considers why it takes some students an unnecessarily long time to reach an adequate standard. Its emphasis is on theory but it provides useful insights for the experienced teacher with some background in applied linguistics and some of the ideas have direct practical implications for classroom activities.

> 2. Randy Quark is an astrophysicist turned popular writer. This latest book marks a new turning point in his career. Designed for scientists who want to write for a wider public, it focuses on many of the 'dos' and 'don'ts' of such writing. Above all, it will show you how to break out of the conventions that too many years in academe may have forced you to adopt.

> 3. Designed for overseas students who are embarking on an academic course in an English-speaking country, this book takes an approach to writing that has been tried out successfully in the classroom. It is intended for students with an intermediate or advanced level of spoken English who probably have experience of academic writing in their own language but whose writing in English may have so far been of a fairly basic kind linguistically and thematically very general.

Task 6

Quickly skim all of the first paragraph and then the first sentence of each paragraph of the following article. Then answer question 1 below the text.

Meadowfoam

Britain's farmers are looking to diversify their operations, as they increasingly 'set aside' surplus cereal-growing land. An unusual new crop being tested in the UK could mean that some farmers will move into cosmetics.

Meadowfoam, a plant native to western Canada and the north-west of the USA, has seeds which consist of up to one-third vegetable oil, which rivals sperm whale oil in quality. With increasing world pressure against commercial whaling, new sources of oil are eagerly sought for the huge cosmetics market in lipsticks, face creams and beauty products. Other oil-producing crops, including coriander, fennel and marigolds, are also likely to appear in UK agriculture.

Meadowfoam was first tested commercially in Oregon in 1985, and trials here have so far had encouraging results. Seed company J K King and Sons of Coggeshall in Essex predicts a commercial acreage in the UK within two or three years. King has joined forces with Croda Universal of Goole on Humberside which has developed a process for 'cleaning up' the raw, green, smelly oil extracted from the seed so that it can go into cosmetics. A trial with the vast Japanese cosmetics industry has been successful.

Meadowfoam oil could also replace sperm whale oil in textile, plastic, surfactant and lubricant manufacture. And because it is easily converted into a liquid, it could take some of the market for shampoos now met by jojoba oil, which is produced mainly in Arizona and New Mexico.

A short-season crop normally sown in October, meadowfoam produces magnificent, foamy white flowers in June and its seeds can be harvested in mid-July. Trial yields of up to 2 tonnes per hectare have been achieved, but new, higher-yielding varieties are being developed at Oregon State University and in the UK.

The plant is catholic in its acceptance of different soils (except very light sands) and seems to cope unusually well with the wet British summer. From the farmer's point of view, harvesting in mid-July means that it can be slotted in before rapeseed harvesting, making it a good proposition.

Coriander seeds have a 17 per cent oil content of which 82 per cent is either petroselenic acid or oleic acid, fatty acids much sought after by industry, and the plant grows well in cool climates. The soap and detergent industry spends vast sums (one estimate for Western Europe alone is £100m a year) importing huge amounts of palm kernel and coconut from tropical countries to extract their lauric acid, but if coriander (and fennel) were grown as a mainstream arable crop, the petroselenic acid could be chemically split to produce lauric acid.

Oleic acid is used as a plastics lubricant and in making cosmetics. It may be possible to split this long-chain fatty acid to produce both lauric acid and a much shorter-chain fatty acid to replace a petrochemical-derived raw material currently used to manufacture nylon and some plastics.

With meadowfoam possibly becoming a feature of the UK lowland agricultural landscape, fields full of frothy flowers could prove to be an attractive part of our future agricultural landscape.

(M. Smith, 'Not just a cosmetic idea', *The Independent*, 23.1.89.)

1. Give three reasons why British farmers might consider growing meadowfoam.

Now read quickly through the whole passage again and answer the following questions, using your own words as far as possible.

2. (a) Why are vegetable oils being considered as replacements for whale oil?
   (b) What two factors make raw meadowfoam oil unsuitable for cosmetics?
   (c) What advantage for the farmer is there in meadowfoam being a short-season crop, harvested in July?
   (d) Why might coriander (and fennel) crops result in a reduction in the importation of palm kernel and coconut?

TASK 7

Introductions (and conclusions) will be examined in Unit 3. In the meantime, the tasks below will give you further practice in surveying material rapidly.

1. Imagine you are interested in finding information on the following:

   (a) How to write an extended academic essay in English
   (b) Similarities between the writing processes of experienced L1 and L2 writers
   (c) How the composing processes of unskilled L2 writers differ from those of unskilled L1 writers
   (d) Why L1 writers write faster than L2 writers
   (e) Why L2 writers are less likely to be skilled than L1 writers

(**Note:** L1 = a person's first or native language
          L2 = a different language, learnt later)

Look at the introduction below from an academic journal article. Decide if you are likely to find information on any of the above in the article which follows this introduction.

> Research on composing by native speakers of English has shown that the processes used by skilled writers can be described and taught in the classroom. Researchers have also examined the composing behaviors of unskilled writers to determine common features and to make recommendations for classroom teaching. While ESL composition research has pointed out the similarities between the processes of experienced L1 and L2 writers, less attention has been directed to unskilled L2 writers and how their composing processes differ from those of unskilled L1 writers. This article attempts to begin to fill that gap. It first examines, from a theoretical perspective, what we know about composing in a first and second language and what we need to know. It then describes a study in which unskilled ESL writers in a 'developmental' college writing course wrote an essay in class. The findings from this study are then compared to those of some major studies of the composing process, and conclusions are drawn about the specific needs of unskilled ESL student writers.

(Ann Raimes, 'What unskilled ESL students do as they write: a classroom study of composing',
TESOL Quarterly, vol. 19, no. 2, June 1985.)

2. The text below is an introduction to an article in a politics journal. On which of the following items could you expect to find information in the article?

(a) The British electoral system

(b) Voting behaviour in one-party states

(c) The effects of a country's electoral system on its politics

(d) The reasons why there is a lack of books and articles dealing with Latin American electoral systems

(e) Comparisons between electoral legislation in Britain and Brazil

Electoral systems are important in at least two ways. First, they have significant political consequences. Electoral systems shape the nature of parties and party systems, and they affect the behavior of politicians and the strategies of voters. For example, in single member district plurality systems, voters have a strong incentive to select one of the two strongest candidates, and politicians have an incentive not to form third parties. Consequently, electoral systems have a strong effect on the number of parties and hence on the nature of competition in the party system. Although the issue has been explored less, electoral systems also affect the ways parties organise and function internally.

Second, electoral systems also reveal interesting information about the predilections of politicians. Once instituted, electoral systems shape politicians' behavior, but politicians may have occasional opportunities to revise electoral legislation, hence to select a system more to their liking. Politicians' preferences about electoral legislation indicate a great deal about how they operate and how they perceive the political system. Whereas the first important aspect of electoral systems refers to their political consequences, this second aspect concerns their political origins.

This paper looks at both the political consequences and the political origins of the Brazilian electoral system. Regarding the former, my basic argument is that several aspects of Brazil's electoral legislation have either no parallel or few parallels in the world and that no other democracy grants politicians so much autonomy vis-à-vis their parties. This electoral legislation reinforces the individualistic behavior of politicians and

has contributed to undermining ef-forts to build more effective political parties. The extremely low degrees of party loyalty and discipline found in the major parties (except-ing several parties on the left) are tolerated and encouraged by this legislation. In turn, limited party discipline and loyalty have contributed to the singular underdevelop-ment of Brazil's political parties.

In addition to analysing consequences of electoral laws, the paper examines the political rationale behind these laws. Electoral systems are almost always instituted and changed as much to protect and favor some interests as to realise an 'ideal' set of electoral laws. Notwithstanding their frequent laments about the weakness of political parties, Brazilian politicians have consistently opted for electoral systems that weaken parties. I argue that they have done so because they perceive measures that could strengthen party discipline as authoritarian, and also in response to their fears that executives would otherwise be able to control them ruthlessly. Finally, their preference for antiparty electoral systems reflects their belief that they can more effectively represent their own clienteles – and get reelected – if party organisations are weak.

Despite the evidence that electoral systems are important, this subject has been neglected in the study of Latin American politics, even as studies of elections, parties, public opinion, and other institutional issues have burgeoned in recent years. Remarkably, there are no books and very few articles in English on electoral systems in Latin America. This paper responds to that lacuna in the study of Latin American politics, focusing on the consequences and origins of the Brazilian electoral system.

(Scott Mainwaring, 'Politicians, parties and electoral systems: Brazil in comparative perspective', *Comparative Politics*, October 1991.)

TASK 8

The title and printing history pages of a book are given below. Decide what information you would record from these if you wanted to refer to the book in the future.

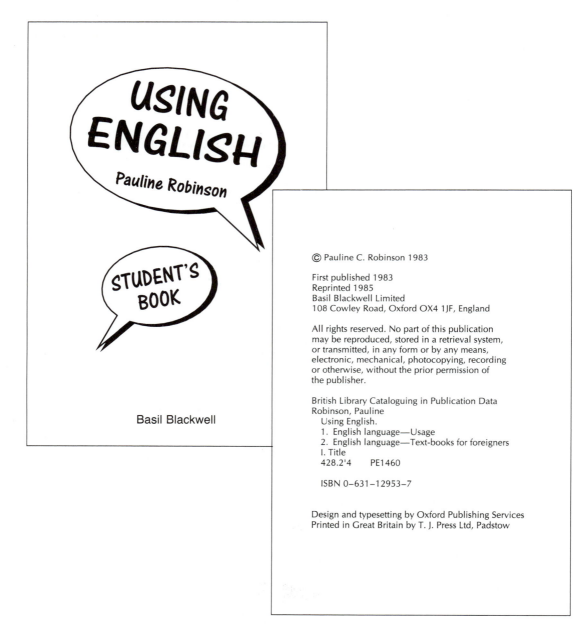

USING ENGLISH

Pauline Robinson

STUDENT'S BOOK

Basil Blackwell

© Pauline C. Robinson 1983

First published 1983
Reprinted 1985
Basil Blackwell Limited
108 Cowley Road, Oxford OX4 1JF, England

All rights reserved. No part of this publication
may be reproduced, stored in a retrieval system,
or transmitted, in any form or by any means,
electronic, mechanical, photocopying, recording
or otherwise, without the prior permission of
the publisher.

British Library Cataloguing in Publication Data
Robinson, Pauline
    Using English.
    1. English language—Usage
    2. English language—Text-books for foreigners
    I. Title
    428.2'4   PE1460

    ISBN 0–631–12953–7

Design and typesetting by Oxford Publishing Services
Printed in Great Britain by T. J. Press Ltd, Padstow

UNIT

2 *NOTE-TAKING AND SUMMARISING SKILLS*

MAIN SKILLS	TASKS CORRESPONDING TO SKILLS
NOTE-TAKING.	TASKS 1, 2 + 3
SUMMARISING IN ONE OR TWO SENTENCES.	TASKS 4 + 9
GLOBAL SUMMARISING.	TASKS 5 (+ 9)
SELECTIVE SUMMARISING	TASK 6
SELECTIVE NOTE-TAKING AND RECONSTITUTION .	TASKS 7 + 8
AVOIDING PLAGIARISM.	TASK 10
SUMMARISING AN ARTICLE	TASK 11

AIMS

This unit aims to revise and practise note-taking and summarising skills. To take notes and summarise information effectively you will need to be able to:

- recognise main, relevant ideas in a text
- extract these ideas and reduce them to note form
- rewrite your notes in a coherent manner in your own words.

NOTE-TAKING

To write effectively you must be able to make effective notes (both of source material and of your own work). You must be able to recognise main or relevant ideas in a text and be able to reproduce these in note form.

Generally speaking, notes from a text are taken for two reasons:

- as a permanent record for later reference
- as relevant or important points to include in your own written work.

When students have to take notes from a book or article, the end product is too often a piece of continuous prose. Sentences or phrases are copied from the original, often with some deletion of less important material.

In exceptional cases, such copying may be necessary (especially when a large amount of concentrated detail from the original is required or when the original writer has expressed ideas so well that they might be suitable for quotation). However, in general, it is not desirable, firstly because plagiarism must be avoided. It is important when you are extracting ideas from a text that you do not use the words of the original or 'lift' chunks of language verbatim (i.e. copying long sections word for word). This is known as plagiarism. Plagiarism is the use of other writers' words or ideas without proper acknowledgement; in other words, literary theft. You must re-express the ideas in your own words. (At the end of this unit, Tasks 10 and 11 draw attention specifically to avoiding plagiarism and focus on how the content of a text may be incorporated into your writing in an acceptable way.)

There is also another important reason for avoiding copying from your source when taking notes. Copying can easily prevent a true understanding of a text, especially if you have some language problems.

You may already be an experienced note-taker in your own language. The next section may still be useful to you, however. It includes several suggestions in the following areas to facilitate note-taking:

1. Selective note-taking
2. Identifying main purposes and functions – global note-taking
3. Identifying main and subsidiary information
4. Using symbols and abbreviations
5. Producing a diagrammatic 'skeleton'
6. Adding to the 'skeleton'
7. Mind maps
8. Note cards.

1. SELECTIVE NOTE-TAKING

It may be that only parts of a text are relevant to your needs and attempting to take notes on all of it will only waste time. In this case, you will have to decide what to *edit in* and what to *edit out* by reading through the text and noting down clearly which parts of it you will need to take notes on. If the text is your own property, it is useful to highlight these parts by underlining or using a highlighter pen.

2. IDENTIFYING MAIN PURPOSES AND FUNCTIONS OF A TEXT – GLOBAL NOTE-TAKING

Whether you require partial information from a text or need to take notes on all of it, identifying its main purposes and functions will be indispensable. Reading the title and introduction of a text should give you an idea of both. As we saw in Unit

1, Task 1, the titles of academic texts are usually informative. In many cases, the purposes and functions of a text may be identical. For example, a text may suggest solutions to a problem, defend reasons for a policy or describe the properties of a material. In other cases, one or several functions may contribute to a purpose; a description and comparison of two methods may serve to show that one of them is better than the other.

Short task

As we saw in Unit 1, looking at the introduction of a book or article (or the first paragraph of a chapter) can help to identify information which may otherwise take a long time to extricate from the main body of a piece of work. For example, look at the following extracts from the introductions of students' extended essays. What purposes and functions are conveyed in them?

(a) 'The purpose of this work is to examine the possible causes of the disease in the light of research that has been carried out in the last decade.'

(b) 'The first objective of this paper is to describe the process by which a solar drier can be used to preserve fruit and vegetables. This is followed by a discussion of the cost-effectiveness of teaching such a technique in the aforementioned areas.'

(c) 'The findings of this study are compared with those of previous well-known studies and some unexpected conclusions are drawn about the needs of new learners.'

(d) 'As suggested in the title, the two solutions to traffic congestion offered in this essay may have their drawbacks but they have met with considerable success in the case studies that are described.'

---

3. IDENTIFYING MAIN AND SUBSIDIARY INFORMATION

When reading the main body of a text you will have to look for indicators of important information that you will want to note down. The easiest type of writing to follow is that in which factual information is presented in a *linear* form. There is little difficulty in identifying a sequence of events or points or the stages of a process, especially when they have been indicated by markers such as *First ... Secondly ... Next ... Finally ....*

In some subject areas the kind of linear presentation described above is very common. However, the majority of texts in many subjects may not have such easily recognisable indicators in presenting information. If there is a lot of discussion, it may be difficult to identify points or distinguish what is more important from what is of secondary importance. Moreover, even if there is a linear form distinguishable in the information, it may be presented in a non-linear way. To take a simple example, it may be possible to distinguish a linearity of time in a text but the sequence of events may not necessarily be mentioned in the order in which they occurred.

Short task

Read the text below and see how it is then presented in note form. When you are taking notes, remember to use the words which carry information (mainly nouns, verbs and adjectives).

Underwater Cameras

Regular cameras obviously will not function underwater unless specially protected. Though housings are available for waterproofing 35 mm and roll-film cameras, a few special models are amphibious – they can be used above or below the water.

  Most of these cameras are snapshot models, but one, Nikonos, is a true 35 mm system camera. Though lenses and film must be changed on the surface, the camera will otherwise function normally at depths down to 70 m. Four lenses are available: two of these, which have focal lengths of 90 mm and 35 mm, will function in air and water; the other two, the 28 and 15 mm lenses, work only under water. Lenses are also available from other manufacturers.

From M. Freeman, *The Encyclopedia of Practical Photography*, London: Quarto Books 1994.

A suggested answer to the short task would look like this:

Underwater Cameras

1. Regular Cameras
   special housing necessary

2. Amphibious
   (a) snapshot models
   (b) Nikonos (35 mm system camera)
       Lenses:
       (i) in air & water – 35 mm
                             90 mm
       (ii) only under water – 28 mm
                               15 mm

As shown in the example above, when taking notes, it is helpful to employ a system of letters and numerals to distinguish main facts or ideas from subsidiary ones. For example, 1. can be followed by (a), (b), (c) and further sub-divisions may be made using small Roman numerals – (i), (ii), (iii), (iv) etc.

4. USING SYMBOLS AND ABBREVIATIONS

A combination of symbols and abbreviations may help in note-taking from written sources. They are indispensable in taking notes from a lecture where speed is essential. It is important to be consistent when using symbols and abbreviations. Below are some suggestions which are commonly used and which you could incorporate into your own note-taking.

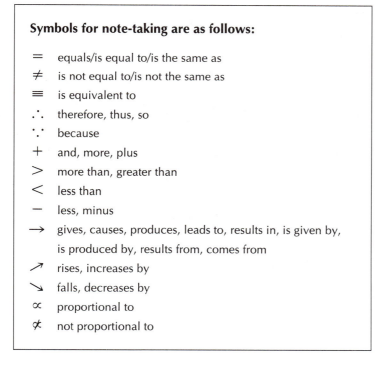

Symbols for note-taking are as follows:

$=$	equals/is equal to/is the same as
$\neq$	is not equal to/is not the same as
$\equiv$	is equivalent to
$\therefore$	therefore, thus, so
$\because$	because
$+$	and, more, plus
$>$	more than, greater than
$<$	less than
$-$	less, minus
$\rightarrow$	gives, causes, produces, leads to, results in, is given by, is produced by, results from, comes from
$\nearrow$	rises, increases by
$\searrow$	falls, decreases by
$\propto$	proportional to
$\not\propto$	not proportional to

Abbreviations for note-taking generally fall into three categories:

1. Common abbreviations, many of them abbreviated Latin terms. For example:
   c.f. (*confer*) – compare
   e.g. (*exempli gratia*) – for example
   etc. (*et cetera*) – and others, and so on
   i.e. (*id est*) – that is to say, in other words
   NB (*nota bene*) – note well
   no. (*numero*) – number

2. Abbreviations used in a particular field of study. For example:
   in chemistry – Au for gold, Mg for magnesium

3. More personal abbreviations, some of which may be words in shortened form that are used fairly commonly. For example:

diff – different
govmt – government
nec – necessary
tho' – although

Notes are made for your own personal use, and, indeed, you may already have developed your own individual style of note-taking. When using abbreviations and symbols, it is important to make sure you will later be able to understand what you have written and that you can reconstitute the notes if necessary. Effective note-taking will enable you to:

• represent important points in brief
• keep a record of important information
• avoid the temptation to plagiarise.

5. PRODUCING A DIAGRAMMATIC 'SKELETON'

You may take notes in a linear form, as in the example on the text about cameras above. However, employing a diagrammatic 'skeleton' to accommodate essential information is useful for two reasons. It can help to clarify your own understanding of the text and it makes it easy to add information later. This may be highly useful when the information that you require is presented in a *non-linear* form in a text. The example below is again based on the text about cameras you saw above: the layout should be far easier to follow than a page of dense prose.

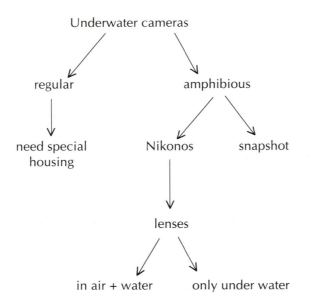

6. ADDING TO THE 'SKELETON'

When you have noted down the essential information, you can then add to your 'skeleton' with details that are less important, or even quotations if necessary. It is therefore important to leave enough space for additional information. Your completed notes are then ready to be referred to in your work or used as the basis for a summary (see next section). In principle, a brief summary (e.g. the abstract of an article) will contain information drawn only from the essential 'skeleton', while a more detailed one may include some less important information too. Deciding what is less important, particularly when there is a lot of detail, is not always easy, but remember to consider how much detail *your* specific needs are likely to require.

7. MIND MAPS

An alternative way of setting down information is to use a 'mind map'. In this case, you write down the central fact or idea in the middle of the page and connect it to other facts or ideas, represented concisely by using 'key words'. A 'key word' is one that is sufficient for you to remember information. If you need detailed information, this technique may be inadequate. However, for the purposes of practising putting ideas into your own words and avoiding plagiarism, its use is highly recommended. (For further ideas on the use of 'mind maps', see Tony Buzan, *Use Your Head*, London: BBC Books, 1989.)

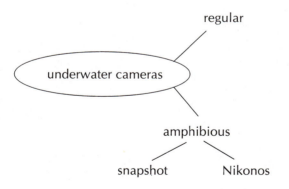

8. NOTE CARDS

Note cards can be used to record important or interesting information. When preparing for a specific research project, it is useful to record one point per card, using one side of the card only. You should record the following information:

- a heading
- one point per card
- identification of source, possibly on the reverse of the card

- page or line reference (for inclusion in references or in case you wish to refer back to the original in the future)
- personal comments on the material.

Information recorded should be in note form and self-sufficient, making it unnecessary later to refer to the source material. In this way you will build a separate, complete and accurate record of important information from source material. When you are writing a paper, it will be easy to select and arrange points in whatever order you wish. Cards can easily be arranged and rearranged to form different sequences and any unwanted cards can be discarded.

There may be occasions when you will wish to record the original wording exactly; for example:

- when the wording of the original is particularly pertinent to an idea you are discussing and cannot be improved upon
- when you wish to quote a particular source to support a line of argument
- to avoid any ambiguity or misrepresentation of source material.

In these cases it is important that you record the exact phrasing and punctuation of the original. You should also indicate on your note card when you have written a quotation as opposed to using your own words.

Now look at an example of note-taking. The notes below are for a paper on 'Native-speaker seminar discourse', by S. C. Levinson, in *Pragmatics*, Cambridge University Press, 1983.

Conversational Analysis (1)
is based on:
(i)   hypothesising sequential expectations based on recurrent patterns in data;
(ii) showing such expectations are participant-oriented;
(iii) showing that while some organis. probs. are resolved by such expectats., others are created.

Levinson, p. 327 (2)

KEY: (1) = heading   (2) = reference

SUMMARISING

In your main course of study, you will almost certainly need to summarise information in writing. You may be required to do this as part of the course or it may prove to be a valuable skill when you are assimilating information for your own further use. Summarising will often be the next step after note-taking in integrating material from sources you have read into your own writing. In fact, the practice of writing summaries from your notes is a useful safeguard against the temptation to plagiarise. Summarising is also an excellent way of ascertaining whether you understand and can remember material you have been reading.

The amount of detail you include in a summary will vary and you may need to be selective in the information you choose to summarise from your reading material. However, you will probably need to go through most of the following stages:

1. Quickly read through the text to gain an impression of the information, its content and its relevance to your work; underline/highlight the main points as you read.
2. Re-read the text, making a note of the main points.
3. Put away the original and rewrite your notes in your own words.
4. Begin your summary. Restate the main idea at the beginning of your summary, indicating where your information is from.
5. Mention other major points.
6. Change the order of the points if necessary to make the construction more logical.
7. Re-read the work to check that you have included all the important information clearly and expressed it as economically as possible.

In a summary you should not include your own opinions or extra information on the topic which is not in the text you have read. You are summarising only the *writer's* information. Also take care not to include details of secondary importance.

Summarising can help you to avoid plagiarism. *It is most important that you use your own words in presenting information (unless you are giving a direct quotation).* It is better to adopt the practice of taking notes and then writing a summary from your notes without having the original text in front of you. In the academic traditions of the English-speaking world, using another person's words and ideas, without indicating that they are not your own, where they came from and who wrote them, provokes a very negative reaction.

Short task

Look at the four ways in which summaries of the source have been attempted by students. Which of these are acceptable as summaries?

Salaries rise in line with fees

Students are borrowing more money to finance college education compared with 10 years ago but, when they graduate, their loan payments are taking up a smaller percentage of their salaries.

One-half of all graduates borrow some money, according to figures from the US Department of Education, up from 34 per cent in 1977. The average debt for recent grauates is $4,800, up from $2,000 in 1977.

The government has been deliberately shifting the emphasis from grants to loans, and more students have been forced to take out loans because of rising fees.

'College students are borrowing more than they did 10 years ago to pay for rising college tuitions,' said Acting Secretary of Education Ted Sanders. 'But when you take earnings into account, debt should not be a hardship for most graduates.'

(a) Students are borrowing more money to finance college education compared with 10 years ago but, when they graduate, their loan payments are taking up a smaller percentage of their salaries.

1/2 of all graduates borrow some money, according to figures from the US Dept. of Education, up from 34% in 1977.

The government has been deliberately shifting the emphasis from grants to loans, and more students have been forced to take out loans because of rising fees.

(b) Students are borrowing more money to finance college education than 10 years ago but, after graduating, their loan repayments are taking up a smaller percentage of their salaries.

50% of all graduates borrow money, according to US Dept. of Education figures, compared with 34% in 1977.

The government has deliberately been shifting

emphasis from grants to loans. More students have been forced to take out loans because of increasing fees.

(c) More money is being borrowed by students to finance college education. Half borrow some money, compared with 34% in 1977, according to US Dept. of Education figures.

The government has emphasised loans rather than grants and rising fees have forced students to take out the former. However, when earnings are taken into account, the debts should not be a hardship for the majority of graduates.

(d) More students (50%) are taking out loans to finance college education than in the past (34% in 1977) due to rising fees, the move away from grants being in line with US Government policy. However, the proportion of earnings needed to repay the money is smaller.

(The Times Higher Educational Supplement, 15.3.91.)

Of the four summaries, (a) is clearly unacceptable as a summary and, if not acknowledged as a quotation, it would be plagiarism. Summary (b) is also unacceptable, even if it changes some of the wording in the original. It has very probably been written by copying from the original. The words have perhaps been changed because the student feels obliged to use his or her own words. This kind of copying or 'modified plagiarism' may disguise students' lack of understanding of a subject or lack of ability to express ideas in their own words. By largely following the vocabulary and sentence patterns of the original, (b) fails as a summary, even if it deletes some less important information.

The author of summary (c) attempts to move away more from the vocabulary and sentence pattern used in the original but too many phrases are 'lifted'. This still suggests that the student might not understand the original fully or has trouble putting the content into her or his own words. Only (d) is satisfactory as a summary, for the following reasons:

- It succeeds in conveying the essential information in fewer words, expressing the content of the six original sentences in two.
- It deletes less important information.
- It departs more freely from the vocabulary and sentence patterns of the original.
- It successfully 'combines across' the paragraphing of the original.

Unlike (a), (b) and (c), the successful summary in (d) has very probably been written from *notes* on the original text rather than from the original itself.

UNIT 2 — *NOTE-TAKING AND SUMMARISING SKILLS: TASKS*

TASK 1

Look at the passage below. Underline/highlight the main points and then reproduce them in note form, using any system you prefer.

> **Romantic Landscape Photography**
>
> Romanticism is one of the most widely popular styles of landscape photography. Within the romantic style there have been many different individual styles which have been more or less fashionable at any one time.
>
> Early pastoral approaches, such as that of George Davies, followed painterly influences and are still popular with some photographers. A certain amount of softness is often deliberately introduced by a number of means. Soft-focused and diffused lenses are an obvious method. Others include shallow focus, soft-printing and the use of fast film for graininess. The subject matter tends to be comfortable, familiar and rural rather than wild and unusual.
>
> Drama and grandeur are other versions of the romantic theme, and are generally more acceptable to modern tastes because they appear to be less contrived and dominated by technique than the pastoral photographs. Yet the apparent impression of spontaneity is often false. Ansel Adams, for instance, visualises his photographs as closely as possible before taking them. This is evident in both the timing and the precision of his composition, which tends to exploit the dramatic potential of views to the full. A more extreme presentation of drama in subjects (such as mountains and deserts), lighting (low sun, dusk and dawn), and design (extreme focal length and high sky-to-land ratios) is common in modern magazine photography.

(From M. Freeman, *The Encyclopaedia of Practical Photography*, London: Quarto Books 1994.)

TASK 2

Read the text on magnesium and then complete the note-taking tasks that follow it.

Out of the oceans and on to faster bicycles

Molecule of the month: magnesium. **John Emsley** examines new benefits of the metal that helps to make our planet green

IN A recent edition of *The Lancet* Dr Mike Campbell of Southampton University suggested magnesium as a treatment for chronic fatigue syndrome, also known as ME or myalgic encephalomyelitis. In a test lasting six weeks, 15 patients were given injections of a gram of magnesium sulphate while 17 others were given only distilled water. Twelve of the 15 on magnesium responded positively, compared with only three of the 17 on water. Patients on magnesium therapy reported having more energy, feeling better and coping more easily with pain.

The research is being followed up to see if those treated continue to improve. Liz Morris, Dr Campbell's research student, has been checking the original patients, and those given the placebo injections. Most of the latter opted for a course of magnesium when the original trials were over.

Magnesium is an essential element for all living things. It is at the heart of the chlorophyll molecule that plants need to trap the sun's energy to make sugar and starch molecules. Our planet is green because magnesium-chlorophyll abstracts the blue and red of sunlight and reflects the green. Plants take their magnesium from the soil, and we take our magnesium directly from plants or indirectly by eating animals that feed on them.

Our daily intake is between a third and half a gram (about one-fiftieth of an ounce). Adults have 25 grams (nearly an ounce) spread throughout their body, with most in their bones which act as a store for magnesium. The metal has three functions: it regulates movement through membranes; it is part of the enzymes that release energy from our food; and it is needed for building proteins. We rarely need to worry about getting enough magnesium, but a deficiency manifests itself as lethargy, irritation, depression and even personality changes.

A normal diet provides enough magnesium, although spirits, soft drinks, sugar and fats contain virtually none. Magnesium is not easily absorbed by our bodies and too much acts as a mild laxative, as we discover when we take Epsom salts (magnesium sulphate) or Milk of Magnesia (magnesium hydroxide). Rhubarb and spinach prevent magnesium being absorbed because the oxalic acid they contain forms a compound with it which we cannot absorb. Cooking does not affect magnesium, although if you throw away the water in which greens are boiled you discard more than half their magnesium.

The rising popularity of certain Yorkshire bitters will also boost the magnesium intake of those who drink it. Dr Tom Coultate, of the South Bank Polytechnic in London, comments in his book *Food* that Webster's Yorkshire Bitter may owe some of its unique taste to the high levels of magnesium sulphate in the water used to brew it. Magnesium salts taste bitter.

Magnesium is the fourth most abundant metal on earth, and there are vast deposits of ores such as dolomite (magnesium calcium carbonate) and carnallite (magnesium calcium chloride). Magnesium salts are leached from the land by rivers and carried to the sea where they remain soluble. This explains why there is 0.12 per cent magnesium in seawater; the oceans hold a trillion trillion tons of it. Production now exceeds 300,000 tons, about half coming from the sea.

The Norwegian company Norsk Hydro extracts magnesium from seawater. According to Charles Duff, the company's UK corporate development manager, most magnesium is used in steel refining to remove sulphur, and to strengthen aluminium, but there is an expanding market for magnesium metal itself. Although it is remembered for its historical role in incendiary bombs and flash bulbs, it does not burn as a bulk metal and magnesium tubes and rods can be welded.

Cyclists are among the first to benefit from this new trend. Last year Phil Anderson, the leader of the Dutch cycle team, rode bicycles with pure magnesium frames in the Tour de France and other races. Frank Kirk, the frame's designer, believes that magnesium gives a better combination of strength and lightness than other metals. A steel frame is nearly five times heavier than a magnesium one, and even aluminium is one and a half times as heavy.

Mr Kirk has shown that if the complete frame is cast as a single component from molten magnesium this avoids welded joints while maximising lightness and strength. His firm, Kirk Precision of Chelmsford, has the world's largest pressure die-casting machine for magnesium components, capable of producing 250,000 cycle frames a year. These are being made for Japanese Muddy Fox mountain bikes and the UK the cycle maker Dawes.

Magnesium is already used for luggage frames, disc drives and camera parts, where lightness is important. By the end of the century, production of this versatile metal is expected to exceed 500,000 tons a year as car makers discover the environmental benefits of magnesium for lighter and longer-lasting vehicles. Mercedes already uses it for seat frames and Porsche for wheels. Reducing the weight of a car not only cuts the amount of fuel it consumes, it also reduces its power to kill in road accidents. And at the end of the vehicle's life, the magnesium can be recycled at little cost.

John Emsley is science writer in residence at the Chemistry Department of Imperial College London and author of 'The Elements' (Oxford University Press, £9.95).

(*The Independent*, 29.4.91.)

Note taking tasks

1. Complete the following notes on the text.

Magnesium

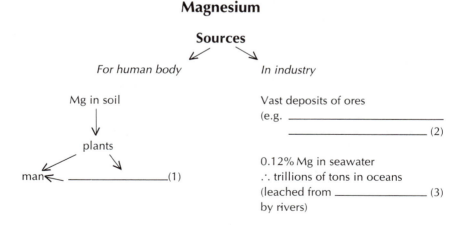

Sources

For human body

Mg in soil
↓
plants
man ← _____ (1)

In industry

Vast deposits of ores
(e.g. _____
_____ (2)

0.12% Mg in seawater
∴ trillions of tons in oceans
(leached from _____ (3)
by rivers)

Properties

An essential _____ (4)
for all living things

At heart of chlorophyll mol.
needed _____ (5) to
trap sun's energy and make sugar &
starch mols

Daily _____ (6) $\frac{1}{3}$–$\frac{1}{2}$ g
Most Mg stored in bones – 25 g
throughout _____ (7)

3 _____: (8)
(i)   regulates movements through
      membranes
(ii) part of enzymes that release
      energy from food
(iii) _____ (9)

Deficiency rare but signs are
lethargy, irritation, depression

4th most abundant metal on earth

(i)   does not burn in bulk
(ii) tubes and rods
      _____ (10)
(iii) _____ (11)
(iv) can be cheaply recycled

Prodn. > 300,000 t (about $\frac{1}{2}$ from
sea)

> _____ (12) per a.
by end of C.

Expanding mkt.

Uses

Medical

Has been successful in treatment of
chronic fatigue syndrome,
according to recent research

Industrial

In steel refining to remove
_____ (13) & strengthen
aluminium

Cycle, luggage, car seat
_____ (14), disc
drives, camera & vehicle parts.

2. Now try representing the information more concisely by completing the 'mind map' started below. Remember to write down key words rather than phrases.

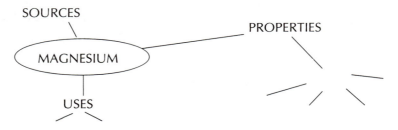

SOURCES

MAGNESIUM

PROPERTIES

USES

SUMMARISING

There are various types of summary you may need to make during your course. Three main types can be distinguished:

1. It may be satisfactory for your needs to summarise a text in only one or two sentences. A short summary like this may be needed, for example, for the abstract of a short essay or article you have written.

2. A more detailed summary may be necessary. For example, you may need to summarise the entire content of an article you are reading. This is called *global summarising*.

3. You may need to summarise only some of the information in a text. Such a selective summary may involve the extraction of relevant material from a large body of prose.

DISCUSSION

If you have an article or chapter of a book in your subject area and need to incorporate many of the ideas into an essay you are writing, which of the following strategies are you most likely to adopt? Discuss them with your teacher.

(a) Translate the text into your own language. You can then make sure you understand it and translate relevant parts back into English (without having to look at the original) when you write your essay.

(b) Having made sure you understand the English, write an acknowledgement of the source of the text at the beginning of your essay. This will allow you to copy freely from the text in your writing and save time and effort in having to put everything into your own words.

(c) Having acknowledged the source of the text, quote all the parts that are relevant to your needs in your writing. It is better to quote than to risk making mistakes by paraphrasing or summarising.

(d) Read through the text, copying sentences or phrases that are relevant to your work but making sure to change some of the wording as far as possible.

(e) Take notes on the text in your own words in English, having made sure you understand it. You can then use your notes in writing your essay without having to consult the original text. The notes can also be used as a basis for a summary of the text if this is needed.

Task 3

Read the text on the following page. Complete the notes that have been started on it and then transfer the information to complete the partial short summary that follows.

When it comes to urban transportation and haulage, it may be a case of 'Back-to-the-Future' for Asian cities. Nonmotorised vehicles (NMVs in the jargon of economists and city planners) account for 25 to 80 per cent of all vehicular transport in many Asian cities. In Shanghai, for example, nearly half the population rides a bicycle, and rickshaws and hand-pushed carts are a widespread sight in most cities in Asia today.

Although the number of cars is increasing at great speed, the number of NMVs also continues to rise. This may be good news for city planners and environmentalists who are trying to cope with pollution and other costs associated with motorised traffic in developing cities. NMVs offer affordable, quick and convenient transportation for trips of short to intermediate distances. They are also ecologically sound, significantly reducing air and noise pollution, petroleum consumption, global warming, and traffic congestion.

Yet, the future of NMVs is at risk unless their use is supported by government policy. As Asian cities continue to grow – most of the world's largest cities are in this region – and as the number of motor vehicles increases, street space for safe NMV use is frequently lost. In addition, credit financing and transport planning often favor motorised vehicles. In Jakarta, for example, bans, fines, and taxes that severely restrict or eliminate rickshaws have been in effect over the past five years.

Nevertheless, support for one transportation mode need not exclude the other. Adopting regulations that support NMV use, while allowing for motor vehicles and pedestrian traffic, is an attainable, realistic goal, as many Asian cities have discovered. This can be achieved by maintaining extensive cycle paths and NMV parking at rail and bus terminals to provide easy access to as many destinations as possible to both drivers and cyclists. Employee commuter subsidies offered to those bicycling to work, and accelerated domestic NMV production are other effective incentives for NMV use.

(From *Finance and Development*, vol. 29, no. 3, September, 1992.)

Notes

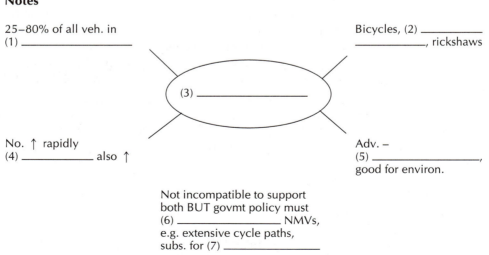

25–80% of all veh. in
(1) _____

Bicycles, (2) _____
_____, rickshaws

(3) _____

No. ↑ rapidly
(4) _____ also ↑

Adv. –
(5) _____,
good for environ.

Not incompatible to support both BUT govmt policy must
(6) _____ NMVs,
e.g. extensive cycle paths,
subs. for (7) _____

Summary

Nonmotorised vehicles constitute between 25 and 80 per cent of all vehicles in many Asian cities in the form of (1)_____. Their number is increasing, though cars are also on the rise. Supporting the two types of transport need not be mutually exclusive. NMVs have the advantage of being good for the (2)_____ and cheap. However, their use must be actively encouraged by (3)_____. For example, (4)_____ should be supported while people who cycle to work can (5)_____.

Task 4

Read the texts below, then summarise the content of each in one or two sentences.

(a) Japan is prone to earthquakes and typhoons. But sound construction, education and communications mean that the people are less vulnerable than citizens of poorer nations. Japan suffered 43 disasters from 1960 to 1981 with an average 63 deaths per disaster; Bangladesh had 63 catastrophes over the same period with an average death toll of over 10,000.

The difference in the killing power of disasters between rich and poor areas is dramatic. A 1972 earthquake in Managua, Nicaragua, killed 5,000 people; whereas the previous year a stronger quake in a similarly densely populated area around San Fernando, California, killed a total of just 65.

As the poor populations of the Third World increase, and as social, political and economic systems force these growing numbers to live on vulnerable ground, they fall foul of catastrophes in increasing numbers. Annual earthquake victims increased by 500 per cent from the 1960s to the 1970s; hurricane victims increased by 12 per cent.

Poverty increases the effect of disasters hundreds-fold, and Bangladesh is one of the world's poorest nations. Over 100 million people live in the delta of two of the world's great rivers; about 15 million of them less than 10 ft above sea-level.

(From L. Timberlake, 'The greatest threat on earth', *The Independent*, 12.9.88.)

(b) Owing to the accident of recent geological history the fauna and flora of Britain itself is in many ways impoverished and still recovering from the last Ice Age; contrast the handful of native tree species here with the thousands in a tropical rain forest, or even the hundreds in the temperate forests of western China. It is the same with many animal groups. For every plant species in its own environment it is estimated that there may be 20 to 30 insects and other animals associated with it. This figure is much higher in a rain forest; the numbers in undisturbed tropical habitats are astronomic. There are estimated to be over 60,000 different species of weevil alone, and scientists can still only guess at the full diversity of insects in the Amazon or Borneo.

(From J. E. Milner, 'Why it is absolutely necessary to go on naming names', *The Independent*, 1.8.89.)

TASK 5

1. Look at the global summaries following the article below. Which do you think are satisfactory? Then discuss the characteristics of effective summaries and important steps in writing them.

Fire stones support catastrophe theory

By David Keys
Archaeology Correspondent

MILLIONS of small fire-blackened stones in Ireland and Scotland are giving support to the theory that northern parts of the British Isles were depopulated by a nuclear winter-style disaster almost 3,200 years ago.

Archaeologists believe the disaster was caused by a huge volcanic eruption in Iceland in 1159 BC. An examination by John Barber, of the Scottish Historic Buildings and Monuments Directorate, and other archaeologists, of these piles of burnt stones has led to the conclusion that hunting, as a major part of the prehistoric economy, declined rapidly after the mid twelfth century BC.

The stones were used in the cooking of meat and other food. Now normally referred to as "pot-boilers", they were the main method of boiling water when metal cauldrons were rare and pottery not strong enough to withstand great heat.

Modern tests have shown that normally it would have taken around three such stones, deposited into the pit of water over a 15-minute period, to bring the water to the boil. Many stones were retrieved, reheated and reused.

However, it is the distribution and dating of these fire-blackened mounds of stones which lends support to claims that an environmental catastrophe struck upland areas of the British Isles.

The earliest burnt mounds date from 2,100 BC and for most of the second millennium BC can be found in permanent settlement sites and temporary hunting camp sites. But in upland areas, as from the mid twelfth century BC, burnt mound material persists only in settlement sites.

Hunting camp sites ceased to occur and archaeologists believe this is linked to the volcanic eruption, which probably destroyed much of upland Britain and led to the demise of many game species and, consequently, to a massive move away from hunting.

Research by Dr Michael Baillie and Dr Martin Munro, of the Palaeoecology Centre at Queens University, Belfast, paved the way for the development of the catastrophic depopulation theory. They discovered, through an examination of tree-ring data, that tree growth slowed dramatically at times of major northern hemispheric volcanic eruptions – including that in Iceland.

It is thought that the eruption, which spewed at least 12 cubic km of volcanic dust into the atmosphere, and the ensuing environmental problems, reduced the population of northern Britain by as much as 90 per cent.

(*The Guardian*, November 1988.)

Summary 1

Tree-ring data research by Baillie and Munro at Queen's University, Belfast, showing that tree growth slowed greatly at times of major northern hemisphere volcanic eruptions, gave rise to a catastrophic depopulation theory. According to this theory, northern parts of the British Isles were depopulated by one particularly large volcanic eruption in Iceland in 1159 BC (Keys, 1988).

There is further support for the theory in the examination by Barber and other archaeologists of mounds of small, fire-blackened stones used extensively by hunters to boil water. Their disappearance after the mid 12th century BC from everywhere but permanent settlement sites in upland areas suggests that the volcanic eruption may have killed off many game species and led to a decline in hunting (Keys, 1988).

Summary 2

The existence of piles of burnt stones has led archaeologists such as John Barber of the Scottish Historic Buildings and Monuments Directorate to conclude that a volcanic eruption in Iceland in 1159 BC led to the decline of hunting in the northern British Isles. The stones were used to boil water for cooking. After the mid 12th century BC, they were confined to permanent settlement sites and not found in temporary hunting camp sites, suggesting that the eruption had destroyed many game species. This is further evidence for the catastrophic depopulation theory put forward after research on tree-ring data by Baillie and Munro of the Palaeoecology Centre at Queens University, Belfast. Their findings revealed that tree growth declined markedly following major volcanic eruptions in the northern hemisphere, such as the one in Iceland (Keys, 1988).

Summary 3

Archaeologists believe that a nuclear catastrophe 3,200 years ago led to the depopulation of northern parts of the British Isles. The disaster caused the blackening of millions of stones which have been found in temporary hunting campsites and permanent settlement sites. After the mid 12th century, hunting camp sites ceased to occur, suggesting huge depopulation (Keys, 1988).

Summary 4

The findings of archaeologists are lending support to the theory that depopulation occurred in the northern parts of the British Isles as a result of a serious catastrophe about 3,200 years ago. It is believed that a huge volcanic eruption in Iceland led to a rapid decline in hunting as an economic activity in prehistoric northern Britain.

An examination of piles of small fire-blackened stones by John Barber of the Scottish Historic Buildings and Monuments Directorate and other archaeologists has revealed that hunting probably ceased after the middle of the 12th century BC. The stones, which were the main means of boiling water and were normally used in threes, were found in permanent settlement sites and temporary hunting sites until the mid 12th century BC. From that time, they persisted only in settlement sites. Archaeologists believe that this is because volcanic eruptions led to the destruction of much of upland Britain and the demise of many game species which, in turn, caused a decline in hunting (Keys, 1988).

Summary 5

A volcanic eruption in 1159 BC in Iceland led to depopulation in northern parts of British Isles, according to the findings of scientists. Archaeologists have found that the absence of millions of small fire-blackened stones, after the middle of the 12th century BC, is evidence of a massive decline in hunting, the stones having been used to boil water by hunters in temporary camp sites (Keys, 1988).

Summary 6

The evidence of archaeologists on the distribution and dating of piles of burnt stones supports the theory that northern areas of the British Isles were depopulated by an enormous volcanic eruption almost 3,200 years ago (Keys, 1988). After the eruption, the stones, which were used to heat water for cooking food, were only found in permanent settlement sites. This suggests that hunting ceased as an activity as animals became extinct. I think this is more conclusive evidence than the previous research on tree-ring data. The research showed that tree growth slowed very markedly when there were large volcanic eruptions in the northern hemisphere. However, tree-ring research may not always be reliable.

CHARACTERISTICS OF AN EFFECTIVE SUMMARY

Look at the summaries above which you considered satisfactory. Which of the following characteristics do you think they have, in order to be effective summaries? Discuss.

(a) The same order of facts and ideas as the original

(b) Similar wording to the original with occasional phrases exactly the same

(c) Different sentence patterns from the original

(d) Additional information, which the original writer omitted but which helps an understanding of the subject

(e) A personal comment on the subject

(f) Simpler vocabulary than the original

(g) Identification of key points in the original

IMPORTANT STEPS IN WRITING AN EFFECTIVE SUMMARY

A good summariser may arrive at the final point *without* being aware of the characteristics you have identified above. They are concerned with the final product rather than the process of reaching it. In writing a summary, which of the following steps do you think are important? Discuss.

(a) Read the whole text through once or twice before writing anything down.

(b) Copy important sentences.

(c) Ask questions about when the text was written and for what purpose in order to get a more detached perspective on it.

(d) Find the main idea(s).

(e) Take notes (or make a mind map).

(f) When writing your summary, put aside the original text and work from your notes, putting information into complete sentences in your own words.

2. Read the following extract from an academic journal article. Then decide which of the summaries of the extract which follow are satisfactory.

EVOLUTIONARY BIOLOGY AND POLITICAL THEORY

Roger D. Masters
Dartmouth College

Human nature has been at the foundation of thinking about politics since the ancient Greek philosophers developed the concept of nature as we know it in the West. As political philosophy is conventionally taught and studied today, however, human nature is no longer the subject of scientific inquiry in the precise sense. Instead of formulating hypotheses and subjecting them to empirical tests, political theory in the twentieth century has generally been viewed as a study of the ideas and history of famous thinkers who wrote about human nature and politics.

The tradition of political philosophy arose and flourished in the hands of thinkers who did not make such rigid distinctions as those now practiced in our universities and our intellectual life. Plato's *Republic* presents an educational curriculum that includes the disciplines we call mathematics, physics, chemistry, and biology, as well as those we consider to be philosophic and political in character. Aristotle wrote as least as widely on matters of biology and physics as on politics or ethics. In both the Lyceum and the Academy, not to mention other ancient schools, the contemporary divisions between scholarly disciplines did not exist.

The irony of the gap between what Snow called the Two Cultures is the proliferation of scientific research that bears directly on political theory (see, e.g., Alexander 1979, 1987; Gruter and Bohannan 1983; Ruse 1986; Wilson 1975, 1978). Evolutionary biology makes possible a deeper understanding of human origins and the emergence of political institutions. Neurophysiology, neurochemistry, experimental psychology, ethology, and ecology provide empirically based information about human nature. In the last generation, the fossil record of human origins has been greatly expanded, and the mechanisms of inheritance (the structure and function of DNA) understood for the first time; and the science of social behavior among animals has been enriched by direct observation in the field, by laboratory experiment, and by theoretical models of natural selection.

Although there is an emerging subfield in political science known as biopolitics (Corning 1986; Schubert 1989; Somit 1976; Thorson 1970; Watts 1984), the study of human nature and politics from the perspective of the life sciences has not yet become an accepted approach in any of the social sciences. It seems fair to assume that this state of affairs is not likely to survive the continued advances in the natural sciences. Over the next generation, barring nuclear war and the demise of advanced civilizations, research in the life sciences will doubtless expand our knowledge and our ability to manipulate biological phenomena. The political process must sooner or later be fundamentally affected by the power to change not only the environment but also the behavior and genetic composition of humans themselves (Blank 1981; Kass 1971).

As a result of these trends, I suggest that a ''naturalist'' perspective is emerging, making it possible to view human politics from a perspective consistent with both the tradition of Western political philosophy and the findings of contemporary biology (Masters 1989a). Rejecting the view that social science will be totally absorbed by (or ''reduced'' to) biology, I presume that human behavior is in many important respects unique in the natural world. But unlike those social scientists who have ignored biology or assumed that its introduction into the study of human behavior is ideologically motivated, my analysis seeks to overcome the gulf between scientific research and human self-awareness.

A more scientific approach to political theory must address the age-old theoretical questions of human nature and the state. Biological research can illuminate our understanding of human nature by considering the foundations of human selfishness and altruism, of our participation in social groups, of human languages and cultures, and of politics itself. The origin of the centralized state can, for example, be explored by linking contemporary theories of natural selection to the study of social cooperation in political philosophy, game theory, and history (Alexander 1979; Margolis 1982; Masters 1983; Schubert 1989; White 1981). Although such an evolutionary perspective on human society has often been attacked as ideologically biased, careful analysis shows not only that evolutionary theory is consistent with a wide range of political opinions but that the denial of a natural foundation of human behavior is itself often ideologically motivated (Caplan 1978; Kaye 1986; Masters 1982).

(*American Political Science Review*, vol. 84, no. 1, March 1990.)

Summary 1

Contemporary political theory is not based on a scientific study of human nature. Though human nature lay at the heart of thinking about politics in ancient times, today's divisions between disciplines ensure that the extensive findings of scientific research in fields such as evolutionary biology, experimental psychology and ethology have so far had little bearing on social science. Though there is a new subfield in political science known as biopolitics, most political theory involves the study of the ideas and history of famous political thinkers. Masters predicts that, in view of continual advances in the natural sciences, a 'naturalist' perspective is appearing which will embrace the findings of contemporary biology. Research in this subject can throw light on many important aspects of human nature that affect political behaviour. For example, the existence of the centralised state may be linked to human behaviour through the study of theories of natural selection.

Summary 2

Biological research will sooner or later have a bearing on political theory and behaviour. The study of the way human beings behave and major discoveries in areas such as the mechanisms of inheritance have led to the possibility of scientific findings being adopted in theoretical and practical politics. Though it might be thought that such findings can be ideologically adopted, analysis indicates that this is not necessarily the case. For example, evolutionary theory may be compatible with a wide diversity of political views (Masters, 1990).

Summary 3

The study of political philosophy has been based on the concepts of ancient Greek thinkers. As a result, it has failed to draw on findings in a wide range of scientific fields which study human nature. This state of affairs is unlikely to continue, as research in the life sciences makes it more possible for us to manipulate the environment and human behaviour. A 'naturalist' perspective may emerge which will view human politics from an angle based on findings in biological research as well as traditional political thinking. Such a biological basis for political theory need not be politically biased (Masters, 1990).

Summary 4

An excessively narrow focus in the field of political theory has ensured the exclusion of valuable insights from many scientific disciplines. Findings in biology might have a significant bearing on political thinking and practice. They could illuminate understanding of human nature and its relation to political systems (Masters, 1990).

Summary 5

It is important to study human nature as well as politics. The ancient Greeks studied every kind of subject and made connections between one subject and another in a way that is not possible today. As the scientific study of human nature progresses, it will be possible to make the kinds of connections between politics and human nature which the Greeks made. The significant change will be that there will be a scientific basis to these connections as well as a theoretical one (Masters, 1990).

Summary 6

Science and politics must be studied apart but the former may have increasingly useful insights for political theory and practice as its range of knowledge expands. Subjects such as neurophysiology, neurochemistry, experimental psychology and ecology can furnish empirically based information about human nature. The subfield in political science known as biopolitics is likely to gain increasing acceptance. Eventually, it might be possible for changes in the environment and in human behaviour to be brought about through political processes. Such changes will have a firm basis, unlike the political theory that has so far been taught and studied (Masters, 1990).

Summary 7

The status of politics as a true science must be reinstated. Since ancient Greek times, it has not been considered on an equal footing with subjects such as mathematics, chemistry and biology. With the widening of scientific disciplines into increasingly specialised subjects, it is likely that a scientific study of politics will become the accepted approach. Such a study will draw on the findings of other subjects while remaining ideologically unbiased. It is through this approach that human society may eventually find a basis on which truly altruistic behaviour can be built (Masters, 1990).

TASK 6

Tasks 3, 4 and 5 have considered summaries of the complete content of texts. However, sometimes what is required is to extract and summarise information about *certain* ideas only. This is called a *selective summary*.

1. Look at the text on page 43. You need to find out about the reasons behind the high numbers of foreign scientists being recruited by Japanese research laboratories. Make notes from the text on this subject.

    Then compare your notes with the following selective summaries and decide which one is the most suitable.

Summary 1

Over 28,000 foreign students are enrolled at university and postgraduate degree courses in Japanese universities, 91 per cent of them coming from nearby Asian countries. Many of these students are studying business and economics but some are on science courses. Many foreign science graduates are being employed by Japanese research laboratories due to the lack of interest in science careers on the part of Japanese graduates. The young Japanese are more interested in high salaries and leisure, neither of which are offered by a career in science research (Greenlees, 1991).

Japan paves way for big foreign influx

By John Greenlees

Overseas student numbers in Japan have soared by 32 per cent in just one year, the ministry of education has revealed. There are now 41,000 foreign students at higher education institutions in the country.

The new figures from the ministry (Monbusho) indicate steady progress towards the government's target of 100,000 foreign students studying in Japan by the end of the decade.

They include students undertaking specialised courses at vocational schools as well as those attending junior colleges, universities and graduate schools. The number of foreign students enrolled for university degree and postgraduate courses now stands at 16,177 and 12,383 respectively.

The University of Tokyo, the country's highest ranked university, and Waseda University, one of the country's top private schools, are the two most popular destinations. One thousand one hundred and sixty-one foreign students are studying at the University of Tokyo and 1,061 foreign students are studying at Waseda University.

The Monbusho's survey shows that 91 per cent of Japan's foreign students are from the nearby Asian countries of China, South Korea and Taiwan. The contingent of 18,063 Chinese students represents the largest national group, accounting for 44 per cent of Japan's total intake of foreign students.

Only 1,180 of Japan's growing number of foreign students are from the United States, a number that the Monbusho would like to see increase. It is also keen to attract more students from the United Kingdom and other European states.

Most of Japan's foreign students are paying their own tuition fees. Only 4,961 students are receiving scholarships from the Japanese government and 1,026 students are sponsored by their own governments.

The most popular courses are related to economics, business and finance, followed by engineering and industrial design.

Record numbers of foreign scientists are also being recruited by Japanese research laboratories to compensate for the shortfall in Japanese graduates interested in taking up careers in science. The lure of higher wages and more attractive working conditions is encouraging many of Japan's best graduates to take up posts in the business sector.

University research is proving an unpopular career option. Low wages, and poor promotion prospects, have discouraged many science graduates from considering careers in academia.

Susumu Tonegawa, one of the few Japanese scientists to be awarded a Nobel prize, has repeatedly criticised the inflexible career structures in Japanese research laboratories. In universities, he says, young scientists spend most of their time as assistant researchers running errands for their professors.

Careers in science are also associated with long hours in poor working conditions. "Science lacks appeal for Japan's affluent, and increasingly leisure-oriented, young people," says lecturer Noboru Oda.

In spite of efforts to popularise science in the nation's schools, many high school graduates entering higher education are rejecting places in science faculties and opting for courses in the arts and social sciences.

(*The Times Higher Education Supplement*, 15.3.91)

43

Summary 2

Japanese Nobel Prize winner Susumu Tonegawa criticised the inflexible career structures in Japanese research laboratories. Young scientists may have to do menial tasks such as running errands for their professors. Moreover, wages are low and working hours long. As a result, fewer Japanese young people are attracted to a science career (Greenlees, 1991).

Summary 3

Record numbers of foreign scientists are being recruited by Japanese research laboratories. This compensates for the shortfall in Japanese graduates interested in science careers. Higher wages and better working conditions are attracting many Japanese graduates to jobs in the business sector.

University research is an unpopular career option. There are low wages and poor promotion prospects. In addition, long hours in poor working conditions have discouraged many science graduates from considering careers in academia (Greenlees, 1991).

Summary 4

The reason why Japanese research laboratories are recruiting record numbers of foreign scientists is that science careers have become less popular for Japanese graduates. Low wages, unattractive working conditions and poor career prospects are discouraging them from entering academic research. Arts and social sciences are proving more popular options for study, and the business sector has become a more attractive career choice (Greenlees, 1991).

2. The task on selective summarising which follows is more difficult than the one above. Read the text on page 45 and then decide which of the five pieces of writing that follow it best summarises the information, relevant to the following title:

   The seriousness of the deforestation problem in the tropics

Summary 1

Tropical forests are rich in biological diversity and hardwood, covering a total of about 3 billion hectares in Africa, Asia and Latin America. Their destruction has reached an alarming rate of around 17–20 million ha a year, leading to loss of resources, plants and animal species, as well as pushing out forest inhabitants. In addition, deforestation has an effect on climate and the environment.

"Among the scenes which are deeply impressed on my mind, none exceed in sublimity the primeval forests ... No one can stand in these solitudes unmoved ..."

These words from Charles Darwin take on new meaning in today's environmentally conscious world. Forests, after all, are the most widespread terrestrial ecosystem. Covering around 30 per cent of the earth's total land area, they play vital roles in natural systems, as well as in economic development.

Forests form an integral component of the biosphere, essential to the stabilization of global climate and the management of water and land. They are home for countless plants and animals that are vital elements of our life-supporting systems, as well as for millions of forest dwellers. They provide goods for direct consumption (including recreational activities) and land for food production. They also represent capital when converted to shelter and infrastructure.

The two main types of forests are tropical, which are rich in biodiversity and valuable tropical hardwood, and temperate, which serve as the world's primary source of industrial wood. The temperate forests (1.5 billion hectares) can be found mainly in developed countries, whereas the tropical forests (both moist and dry, totalling about 1.5 billion ha. each) stretch across the developing world. Two thirds of the tropical moist forests are in Latin America, with the remainder split between Africa and Asia; three quarters of the tropical dry forests are in Africa.

But in recent years, there has been an alarming increase in destructive deforestation and land degradation in developing countries, reflecting the earlier development experiences of industrial countries, when large areas of the world's temperate forests were cleared for agriculture, timber and fuelwood. Recent studies show that deforestation, especially in the tropics, has risen to an estimated 17–20 million ha. annually – almost equivalent in area to the United Kingdom or Uganda – from around 11.4 million ha. in 1980. Those hardest hit include Costa Rica, Cote d'Ivoire, Ghana, Honduras, India, Nepal, Nigeria, Thailand, and the Philippines. In the temperate region, old-growth forests are also at risk. Furthermore, forest degradation, largely from acid precipitation, is harming large areas of temperate forests, especially in Eastern Europe.

Already, the misuse of forests has brought with it significant social, economic and environmental costs. Many developing countries, especially in Africa and South Asia, face acute shortages of fuelwood, fodder, timber, and other forest products, not to mention the displacement of their forest dwellers. There has also been a loss of biological diversity, possible global climate change, degradation of watersheds, and desertification. The loss of tropical moist forests is especially worrying, as they provide habitats for more than 50 per cent of the world's plants and animal species, generate genetic materials for food and medicine, and influence the climate, both at the regional and global level.

In recent years, with an increased understanding of – and concern about – the environmental consequences of destructive deforestation, people all over the world have expressed a desire for the sustainable use of forests. But there are strong differences of opinion among people, as well as among nations, about how best to balance conservation and development goals. Further complicating matters is the fact that in industrial countries, there is increasing concern for environmental and preservation considerations and the aesthetic qualities of forests, whereas in developing countries, where people are striving to achieve economic development, forests are frequently seen as a source of food, raw material and capital. The world community must find a way of reconciling these diverse interests in order to create incentives and values that will foster the wise use of forests. The challenge is twofold: to stabilize existing forests by arresting destructive deforestation and to increase forest resources by planting trees.

(From Narendra Sharma and Raymond Rowe 'Managing the world's forests', *Finance and Development*, June 1992.)

Summary 2

The loss of the tropical rain forests, which can be classified into moist and dry, is undoubtedly serious cause for concern. It is all the more alarming when one considers that these forests are to be found in the developing world. The developed countries went through a period of deforestation on the path to industrialisation but their populations were much smaller than that of the developing world today. Moreover, the rate of loss (estimated at 17–20 million ha a year) is very high today. The repercussions on shortages of resources as well as unwarranted climatic and environmental changes may be more far-reaching than we are willing to imagine.

Summary 3

Tropical rain forests are the habitat of numerous animal species and plants. They are also the source of products such as timber and fuelwood. It is therefore alarming to witness their disappearance at a rate of 17–20 million ha a year. Not only is such a loss the cause of depletion of valuable biological richness and resources, but it may also contribute to climatic and environmental changes.

Summary 4

Tropical forests can be divided into two types: dry forests cover around 1.5 billion hectares, mostly in Africa, while moist forests, covering a similar area size, extend over Africa, Asia and principally Latin America.

Deforestation in tropical areas has in recent years proceeded at an alarmingly high rate. An annual rate of loss of as many as 17–20 million hectares represents an area almost as large as the UK.

The costs are high in economic, social and environmental terms. Some parts of the world, notably countries in Africa and southern Asia, can expect to experience serious shortages in products that come from the forest, such as fuelwood, timber and fodder. Tropical moist forests are the homes of over 50 per cent of the world's animal species and plants, also producing genetic materials for medicine and food. In addition, tropical deforestation may have effects on climate, just as acid rain is harmful to temperate forests.

Summary 5

Deforestation increased substantially, from around 11.4 million ha a year in 1980 to around 17–20 million ha by 1992 and was particularly serious in the tropics. It led to severe shortages of forest products such as timber and fuelwood as well as displacing the inhabitants of forests. In addition, it threatens plant and animal species, especially in tropical moist forests where 50 per cent of them are found. Destruction of tropical moist forests also causes loss of genetic material for food and medicine and changes to climate.

TASK 7

Read the passage below and do the activities that follow.

The Importance of Women in Development

In recent years, there has been an increasing recognition of the contribution of women to economic development around the world. On the one hand, it is evident that calculations of national productivity fail to include the existing contribution of women to a country's welfare. On the other, there is a growing awareness that improved conditions for women are fundamental to improvement in overall living standards.

The unregistered contribution to economies of work performed by women is enormous. All over the world, women may provide as many unpaid health services as the formal health sectors in their countries. In Africa, they are largely responsible for food growing (accounting for at least 70 per cent of staple food production in the Sub-Saharan part of the continent), as well as participating in other activities in the agricultural sector (such as raising livestock, marketing and food processing). As pointed out in a UN report (1985), women represent half the world's population, work two-thirds of the world's working hours but earn only one tenth of what men earn. Furthermore, they own as little as one hundredth of the property owned by men.

Education is the key to improving conditions for women. It leads to wider employment opportunities and better information on how to improve the welfare of families. Both developments contribute to a reduction in fertility. The cost of caring for children is inclined to rise, which tends to encourage smaller families with healthier children rather than large ones. Greater awareness of the need for family planning and for better infant nutrition also tends to reduce fertility. Statistics suggest strongly that increases in the literacy of women have led to declining fertility rates in almost every country in the world. In the period 1965–85, the only area in the world which did not witness a falling birth rate while experiencing improved literacy for its female population was Sub-Saharan Africa, where there was an increase of 1.5 per cent in the fertility rate.

Many governments have accepted the importance of investing in improved education for women in order to bring about changes in health, population growth and economic performance. However, even in those places where equal opportunity is actively pursued, there is still a lot of room for improvement. Women continue to be unpaid or underpaid for the work they do, to be constrained in the kind of work they can do and to reach lower levels of attainment educationally than men. In countries where women constitute a large part of the agricultural labour force and are involved in managing production, they may have less access to information, technology and credit than men. These problems are largely due to the persistence of traditional constraints. The result is that resources are inefficiently used, production is sub-optimal and the overall welfare of a society continues to be depressed.

(Source of statistics: 'State of the world's women', 1985; compiled for the UN by New Internationalist Publications, Oxford, UK)

(a) Give a brief oral summary of what you consider to be the most important information.

(b) Take notes on the important information.

(c) Use your notes to write a summary of the text.

TASK 8

Read the passage below and then do the following:

(a) Produce a set of notes on:
   (i) Criticisms levelled at the TFAP
   (ii) Possible responses to the criticisms.

(b) Reconstitute your notes in the form of two short paragraphs. Remember to use your own words. Do not refer to the original text but only your notes when writing the paragraphs.

The billion dollar question marks

Damien Lewis

THE much-maligned Tropical Forestry Action Plan (TFAP) of the United Nations Food and Agriculture Organisation meets in Rome next week to discuss the findings of an independent review. How it responds to the criticisms levelled at it could determine the future of the tropical forests.

Launched earlier this year, the review – commissioned at the request of the FAO – has been assessing the performance of the TFAP over the past five years and considering criticism from a wide variety of sources.

The team of three external consultants will present a number of possible options ranging from scrapping the TFAP altogether, to doing nothing. Any changes made will be crucial because the TFAP is now facing a barrage of opposition, not only from green groups but from major funding sources.

Linda Chalker, British Minister for Overseas Development Aid, has recently stated that the Plan 'needs reform', and that she would 'not let up on the pressure to change it'.

The TFAP was dreamed up in 1984 when a group of top foresters realised that the past decade of forestry aid had done little to tackle deforestation in the Tropics, and that drastic action was required. A year later the World Bank, the United Nations Development Programme, the World Resources Institute and the FAO joined forces to set it up. The TFAP, they decided, would be a multi billion dollar 'global tropical forest conservation and development programme to stimulate financial commitment from developing and industrialised countries, development assistance agencies and the private sector'.

The idea was that it would not be a rigid plan so much as a strategy, an attempt to identify priorities and create a framework for action. Initially, government would request assistance from the FAO, following which a national forestry plan would be drawn up for that country. Bilateral aid agencies, like Britain's Overseas Development Administration, and multilateral agencies like the Asian Development Bank, would then select specific projects from within these national plans to fund.

In one sense, the TFAP has been very successful; since its launch 76 countries – whose territories include most of the remaining tropical forests – have signed up or are showing interest. In the past five years, 40 major national and international aid agencies have channelled funding through the TFAP, and helped boost forestry aid to more than $1 billion a year – double its figure in 1985.

Yet those opposed to the TFAP point out that this increased TFAP-related activity may actually be causing accelerated deforestation in the tropics. Critics from the 'forestry camp' include John Blower, who has spent 20 years managing various FAO forest conservation projects. He concludes that 'while TFAP documents may have environmental conservation lip-service written in, the general thrust is commercial, aimed at the immediate improvement of the recipient country's economy'.

The most outspoken critics of the TFAP are now the World Rainforest Movement and Friends of the Earth, who stated in a report published earlier this year that 'deforestation seems likely to increase under the TFAP… with logging substantially increased in primary forest areas'. Looking more closely at individual national plans they pointed out that 'the Peruvian plan will dramatically accelerate the rate of deforestation … the Guyanese will accelerate forest degradation through a massive increase in logging and the Cameroon Plan will cause major deforestation'.

However, after this series of apparently disastrous national plans, two have now emerged (Papua New Guinea and Tanzania) which have so far received guarded approval. The Papua New Guinea plan has been hailed by Linda Chalker as proof that 'the TFAP can be effective'. For the past decade in Papua New Guinea, Japanese logging companies have been decimating the forests, but the TFAP has now called for a moratorium on all new logging licences and a review of present logging activities. The government is now

appealing to the international community for compensation for lost timber revenues, and funding for a national system of protected forest areas.

It remains to be seen if these more radical plans will receive adequate funding. Meanwhile, most of the nine national plans now completed are still meeting severe criticism. Simon Counsell of Friends of the Earth argues that 'all UK and international funding should be halted, until a thorough and independent review of the TFAP has taken place', and adds that 'it is time the Food and Agriculture Organisation went back to the drawing board'.

The key question is whether next week's review will address the major problems. If the TFAP is to survive, the Rome meeting will have to come up with the solutions that its many critics are looking for. This will involve improving the conservation element of the plan, respecting the needs of indigenous communities, promoting plantations of native tree species in degraded forests as opposed to logging fresh areas, developing sustainable non-wood forest products (such as nuts, fruits and oils), and increasing the involvement of the environmental and indigenous groups in the whole process.

One of the review team's most promising proposals is that the TFAP should be brought under a new world environmental forestry body, to be known as the 'Global Forestry Organisation', which would be a conservation and environmental group-driven agency for the TFAP. If this option were adopted, then it might draw organisations like Friends of the Earth and other green groups into the TFAP.

With only 0.2 per cent of tropical timber production coming from sustainable sources, and tropical deforestation now running at almost double the rate of 1979, an effective solution to the destruction has never been more needed than at present. As the only organisation of its kind, the TFAP possesses enormous potential, both for the destruction of the tropical forest biome, or its future conservation. It now stands at a crossroads where it may either choose to adopt the deeper shade of green that our new age seems to be calling for, or entrench itself in past mistakes and failures.

(*The Guardian*, 8.6.90.)

TASK 9

(a) Divide into groups. Each group will be given one section of a text. Discuss the content of your section, then summarise in one or two sentences.

(b) Form new groups, each containing one member from each of the original groups. Your new group should now have summaries of all the separate sections necessary to make a complete text. This is called a *jigsaw* summary. Arrange the information you have into a logical order.

(c) Make any changes necessary to produce a coherent summary. You will need to consider such things as grammar, reference and cohesion.

TASK 10

1. Read the following text.

Vitamins

The discovery and isolation of many of the vitamins were originally achieved through work on rats which had been given diets of purified proteins, fats, carbohydrates and inorganic salts. Using this technique, Hopkins in 1912 showed that a synthetic diet of this type was inadequate for the normal growth of rats, but that when a small quantity of milk was added to the diet the animals developed normally. This proved that there was some essential factor, or factors, lacking in the pure diet.

About this time the term 'vitamines' derived from 'vital amines', was coined by Funk to describe these accessory food factors, which he thought contained amino-nitrogen. It is now known that only a few of these substances contain amino-nitrogen and the word has been shortened to vitamins, a term which has been generally accepted as a group name.

Although the discovery of the vitamins dates from the beginning of the twentieth century, the association of certain diseases with dietary deficiencies had been recognised much earlier. In 1753 Lind, a British naval physician, published a treatise on scurvy proving that this disease could be prevented in human beings by including salads and summer fruits in their diet. The action of lemon juice in curing and preventing scurvy had been known, however, since the beginning of the seventeenth century. The use of cod-liver oil in preventing rickets has long been appreciated, and Eijkmann knew at the end of the last century that beri-beri, a disease common in the Far East, could be cured by giving the patients brown rice grain rather than polished rice.

Vitamins are frequently defined as organic compounds which are required in small amounts for normal growth and maintenance of animal life. But this definition ignores the important part that these chemical substances play in plants, and their importance generally in the metabolism of all living organisms.

(From P. McDonald *et al*, *Animal Nutrition*, London: Clowes, 1981.)

Look at the ways in which *parts of the text* have been incorporated into the writing of eight pieces of work by students. Decide which of these extracts would *not* be acceptable in writing in an English-speaking academic environment, and why. (**Note:** One of the extracts has some grammatical errors.)

Extract 1

Although the discovery of vitamins dates from the beginning of the twentieth century, the association of certain diseases with dietary deficiencies had been recognised much earlier. In 1753 Lind, a British naval physician, published a treatise on scurvy proving that this disease could be prevented in human beings by including salads and summer fruits in their diet. The action of lemon juice in curing and preventing scurvy had been known, however, since the beginning of the seventeenth century.

Extract 2

Vitamins were discovered in the early part of the twentieth century, the term 'vitamines' having been invented by Funk and later shortened to its present form. However, it had been known, in some cases for more than a century, that certain deficiencies in diet could lead to disease. For example, it was known that cod-liver oil could prevent rickets, while lemon juice was used against scurvy. In the latter case, further evidence was provided in 1753 by the publication of a treatise by a British naval physician named Lind, who proved that a diet including salads and summer fruits was effective in preventing scurvy.

Extract 3

The term *vitamines* was invented by Funk to describe food factors that he thought contained amino-nitrogen. It is now known that only a few of these substances contain amino-nitrogen and the word has been shortened to *vitamins*. Although their discovery dates from the beginning of the twentieth century, the association of certain diseases with dietary deficiencies had been recognised a long time before.

Extract 4

Some background to the discovery of vitamins is provided by McDonald *et al.* in *Animal Nutrition* (1981). Many vitamins were discovered and isolated through work on rats which had been given diets of purified proteins, fats, carbohydrates and inorganic salts. Using this technique, Hopkins in 1912 showed that a synthetic diet of this type was inadequate for the normal growth of rats, but that when a small quantity of milk was added to the diet the animals developed normally. This proved that there was some essential factor, or factors, lacking in the pure diet.

Extract 5

It is not uncommon to take for granted a definition of vitamins which is essentially incomplete. 'Vitamins are frequently defined as organic compounds which are required in small amounts for normal growth and maintenance of animal life. But this definition ignores the important part that these chemical substances play in plants and their importance generally in the metabolism of all living organisms' (McDonald, 1981).

Extract 6

Despite the discovery of vitamins date from the beginning of twentieth century, it had been recognised much earlier the association of certain diseases with dietary deficiencies. In 1753 Lind, a British naval physician, published a treatise on scurvy proving that this disease could be prevented in human beings by including salads and summer fruits in their diet. The action of lemon juice in curing and preventing scurvy had been known, however, since the beginning of the seventeenth century.

Extract 7

As noted by McDonald (1981), certain diseases were associated with dietary deficiencies long before vitamins were discovered (at the beginning of the twentieth century). At the end of the nineteenth century, Eijkmann knew that beri-beri, which was common in the Far East, could be cured by feeding people with brown rice instead of polished rice. As far back as 1753, Lind, a physician working in the British Navy, observed that inclusion of summer fruit and salad in a diet could prevent scurvy.

Extract 8

In the early part of this century, it was shown by Hopkins that rats that were given a synthetic diet of purified proteins, fats, carbohydrates and inorganic salts would not grow normally. However, if a small amount of milk was added, growth would be normal, indicating that some important ingredient was missing in the pure diet (McDonald, 1981).

2. Read the following text quickly.
    Then look at the ways in which eight students used the ideas in different parts of the text in their own writing. Which of the extracts from students' writing would be *acceptable* in academic writing in an English-speaking academic environment? (**Note:** One of the extracts below contains language errors.)

GOVERNMENT aid to industry in the industrial countries increased substantially between 1973 and 1983 and measures to influence trade – largely non-tariff barriers against imports – proliferated. Since then the industrial countries' direct subsidisation of some industries may have declined, but they have significantly increased their use of non-tariff barriers to trade,* perhaps using such barriers as a substitute for domestic industrial policy measures.

Industrial policy can be broadly defined as the deliberate attempt by a government to influence the level and composition of a nation's industrial output. Thus defined, it encompasses a wide variety of government actions, including those to improve the industrial infrastructure and to enhance national labor mobility and efficiency. This article takes a somewhat more limited view, being concerned mainly with government actions to foster specific industries, either so as to shift resources to activities that will use them more productively in support of adjustment goals, or to maintain resources in existing activities for security, political, or other reasons. The focus is thus largely on the more defensive aspects of such policies.

Industrial policies are implemented both through domestic measures such as subsidies and tax incentives, and through trade actions, such as tariffs and quantitative restrictions. The article looks both at policies' domestic effects and at how they may affect trade flows, in particular those of developing countries.

Reasons for the policies

Over the past 15 years, many governments have become increasingly concerned to shape the structure of industry and to ease the burden of industrial adjustment. A number of factors, including the inflationary environment of the early 1970s; the oil shocks and rising commodity prices; slower economic growth, which persisted into the early 1980s; the new capacity in developing countries which added to excess capacity in many traditional industries, such as shipbuilding and steel, in industrial countries; the generally fiercer international competition; and the advent of new technologies played a role in pressing the need to transform the manufacturing sector. This continuing transformation led to concerns about the costs of change and disparities in income between national growth centers and regions in which traditional industries are located. Concerns also emerged about the continued viability of industries considered essential to the national interest.

(From Clemens Boonekamp, 'Industrial policies of industrial countries', *Finance and Development*, vol. 26, no. 1, March 1989.)

*Non-tariff barriers – this term is used to describe all protection measures other than tariffs. It includes measures such as imposing quality restrictions on imports or insisting that importers have a special licence to buy imports.

Extract 1

Government aid to industry in the industrial countries increased substantially between 1973 and 1983 and measures to influence trade – largely non-tariff barriers against imports – proliferated. Since then, the industrial countries' direct subsidisation of some countries may have declined, but they have significantly increased their use of non-tariff barriers to trade, perhaps using such barriers as a substitute for domestic industrial policy measures.

Industrial policy can be broadly defined as the deliberate attempt by a government to influence the level and composition of a nation's industrial output.

Extract 2

For long time industry has been seen as essential for development. Governments may try influence industry in its countries, this happens in the industrial and the developing country. A number of factors, including the inflationary environment of the early 1970s; the oil shocks and rising commodity prices; slower economic growth, which persisted into the early 1980s; the new capacity in developing countries which added to excess capacity in many traditional industries, such as shipbuilding and steel in industrial countries; the generally fiercer international competition; and the advent of new technologies played a role in pressing the need to transform the manufacturing sector. It was necessary the change of structure of industry for governments.

Extract 3

Industrial policy can be broadly defined as the deliberate attempt by a government to influence the level and composition of a nation's industrial output. Thus defined, it encompasses a wide variety of government actions, including those to improve the industrial infrastructure and to enhance national labour mobility and efficiency. This essay will consider only a few aspects of policy. It will concentrate on policies for specific industries.

Extract 4

A broad definition of industrial policy would include a wide number of government actions, ranging from efforts to improve the industrial infrastructure of a country to actions designed to promote specific industries. The latter may involve shifting resources to more productive activities or making sure they remain in existing activities, for example, for security reasons.

Industrial policies may take the form of domestic measures like tax incentives or trade measures such as tariffs. In recent years, non-tariff barriers to trade have been increasingly implemented in industrial countries, possibly as a substitute for domestic measures.

Extract 5

During the past 15 years, many governments have become increasingly concerned to shape the structure of industry and ease the burden of industrial adjustment. Factors such as excess capacity in traditional industries, fiercer international competition and slower economic growth have been important in pressing the need to transform the manufacturing sector. This continuing transformation led to concerns about the costs of change and disparities in income between national growth centres and regions in which traditional industries are located.

Extract 6

There has in recent years been a growing tendency for governments in both industrialised and developing countries to influence the shape and structure of industry in their countries. Boonekamp (1989) cites factors such as 'the inflationary environment of the early 1970s; the oil shocks and rising commodity prices; slower economic growth, which persisted into the early 1980s; the new capacity in developing countries which added to excess capacity in many traditional industries, such as shipbuilding and steel, in industrial countries; the generally fiercer international competition; and the advent of new technologies'.

Extract 7

As Boonekamp has noted, government aid to industry in the industrial countries increased considerably in the years between 1973 and 1983 and measures designed to affect trade also grew rapidly, particularly in the form of non-tariff import barriers. The use of the latter may often have been adopted to substitute for domestic measures of industrial policy.

Extract 8

Boonekamp (1989) noted that aid to industry increased substantially between 1973 and 1983. Measures to influence trade – largely non-tariff barriers against imports – proliferated. Since then, the industrial countries' direct subsidisation of some industries may have declined, but they have significantly increased their use of non-tariff barriers to trade, perhaps using such barriers as a substitute for domestic industrial policy measures.

TASK 11

This task is particularly important as preparation for your final extended piece of academic writing at the end of Unit 5. The task aims at practising the skills discussed in this and previous units and should be done individually.

Select a topic that you are interested in from your subject area. Ideally, it should be a topic related to the one you will write about as the final task at the end of this book. If you have access to a main library or department library, select an article on this topic from a journal or from a book with articles by different people (which will have an editor). Then do the following tasks:

(a) For the article you have selected, write:
  • the essential bibliographic information
  • a note card.
(b) Write a summary of the article you have chosen.
(c) Justify your choice of article very briefly (i.e. on what basis did you select this article?). Include mention of such information as the author, the date of publication, the importance of the subject matter. If necessary, use Unit 1, 'Surveying material', to help you.

UNIT 3

WRITING SKILLS

MAIN SKILLS	TASKS CORRESPONDING TO SKILLS
REPORTING, WRITING REFERENCES AND QUOTATIONS.	TASKS 1, 2, 3 + 4
DIVIDING A TEXT INTO PARAGRAPHS.	TASKS 5 + 6
WRITING INTRODUCTIONS AND CONCLUSIONS .	TASKS 7, 8, 9 + 10
SYNTHESISING INFORMATION FROM MORE THAN ONE SOURCE	TASKS 11 + 13
CONTRASTING AND COMPARING.	TASK 12

AIMS

The aim of Unit 3 is to ensure that you are familiar with the following skills and to help you become proficient in using them:

- incorporating references and quotations in a paper
- paragraph writing
- writing introductions and conclusions
- extracting information or ideas from more than one source and synthesising them into an essay.

REPORTING, REFERENCES AND QUOTATIONS

The inclusion of references and quotations in academic work is an important part of your writing, particularly in research work. At the end of the last unit, you briefly considered ways in which this could be done legitimately. We shall now look at this in greater detail. References and quotations should be included for the following two main reasons:

1. They indicate to the reader the range, extent and nature of source materials you have used to support or challenge the ideas discussed in your work. They show you have read up on your subject area and are able to select appropriate materials.

2. They are an acknowledgement that parts of your work are derived from the material of others and indicate how you have developed your particular approach.

There are two basic methods of acknowledging source materials: by reporting through paraphrase or by direct quotation. Footnotes are used to provide additional explanations or details of work.

REPORTING USING PARAPHRASE

Reporting uses paraphrase (i.e. expressing the ideas of an author in your own words) to acknowledge another author's ideas. You can extract and summarise important points, while at the same time making it clear from whom and where you have got the ideas you are discussing. This is not the same as copying verbatim (exactly word for word) and without acknowledgement.

For example:

Brown (1983: 231) claims that a far more effective approach is …

Brown is the name of the author (always refer to the surname), and the information in brackets refers to the year and page number of the publication quoted, details of which should be presented in the bibliography at the end of your essay. Generally you should put the year in brackets after the surname but variations on this form are possible. It is useful but not essential to give page numbers. In some disciplines, it is common to give only the page number in brackets after the author's name. You will have to check this with your department.

Some other common phrases that could be used include:

In an article/a study by X, …
As X points out, …
X has expressed a similar view.
A study by X indicates that …
X has drawn attention to the fact that …
X claims that …
X found/discovered that …
Research by X suggests that …
X argues that …

Above, you see some examples of reporting verbs, e.g. *claims, points out, has drawn our attention to*. These words may be attitudinal in nature; that is, the choice of a particular reporting verb will often indicate what sort of attitude *you*, as the writer, have about the idea or information you are reporting and its relative importance to the content of your paper. Therefore, it is important to make sure you are fully aware of the meaning and the level of emphasis of the verbs you choose. You will also find it of value to collect your own examples of reporting verbs from your reading.

Short task

Look at the text below to find examples of the kind of phrases listed above and other examples of reporting verbs.

Survival language skills or business needs are not the only compelling reasons for learning a second language. Neurolinguistic research is beginning to suggest that people who know more than one language make use of more of the brain than monolinguals do (Albert and Obler, 1978). Though the evidence is scant, it appears that the part of the brain that is used in second language functioning remains undeveloped in monolingual brains. Albert and Obler (1978) reviewed a series of post-mortem studies on polyglot brains – brains of people who spoke from three to twenty-six languages – and found that certain parts of these brains were especially well developed and markedly furrowed.

Psycholinguistic studies further indicate that people who control more than one language are verbally more skilful than monolinguals, and they mature earlier with respect to linguistic abstraction skills. Lerea and Laporta (1971) and Palmer (1972) report, for example, that bilinguals have better auditory memory than monolinguals, and Slobin (1968) found that bilinguals are better at intuiting meaning from unknown words. Feldman and Shen (1971) discovered that low-income bilingual children were better at learning new labels than low-income monolinguals, and Peale and Lambert (1962) concluded that ten-year-olds who spoke both French and English demonstrated higher skill in linguistic abstraction than their monolingual counterparts. Expanding mental abilities, therefore, may be reason enough to learn a second language.

(From Heidi Dulay, Marina Burt and Stephen Krashen, *Language Two*, Oxford University Press, 1982. Reproduced by permission of Oxford University Press.)

REFERENCE TO SOURCE

This is similar to reporting except that here the authors' names are given in brackets only and are not referred to directly in the text.

For example:

Several researchers have testified to the limitations of this method (Koo, 1985; Manson, 1961; Watkins, 1979).

A previous report (Blake, 1977) indicates the importance of such prior knowledge.

Note also the example in the second sentence of the extract in the short task above. Again, full details of the work of authors mentioned should be given in the bibliography.

DIRECT QUOTATION

It may be desirable to quote the original author's exact words. If you do so, keep the quotations as brief as possible and only quote when you feel the author expresses an idea or opinion in such a way that it is *impossible* to improve upon it or when you feel that it captures an idea in a particularly succinct and interesting way. For example:

The audiolingual approach to language learning is summed up succinctly by Alexander (1968): 'Listen before you speak, speak before you read, read before you write'.

Direct quotations (i.e. using the *exact* words of another author) are used in the following instances:

- when the wording of the original is particularly pertinent to an idea you are discussing and cannot be improved upon
- when you wish to quote an accepted authority to support a line of argument
- to avoid any ambiguity or misrepresentation of source material.

When you are using a direct quotation of a single phrase or sentence, single quotation marks should be used around the words, which must be quoted *exactly* as they are in the original. However, note the following:

- You may wish to omit some of the author's original words which are not relevant to your writing. In this case, use three dots (…) to indicate where you have omitted words.
- The material quoted may already contain a quotation. Here it is necessary to change the single quotation marks ('…') in the original to double quotation marks ("…") to indicate that these were the author's quotation marks and not yours.

Apart from the changes in quotation marks mentioned above, you should reproduce exactly the punctuation and spelling of the original. Longer quotations, of more than three lines, should be indented as a separate paragraph with no quotation marks, as in the following examples.

Leftwich's resource allocation definition of politics is somewhat broader than a power conception, so it may be more vulnerable to the criticism that it collapses the distinction between the political and the social. His original formulation of that definition was:

> Politics consists of all the activities of cooperation and conflict, within and between societies, whereby the human species goes about obtaining, using, producing and distributing resources in the course of the production and reproduction of its social and biological life.[29]

Hoffman singles out this definition as exemplifying the problem of how broad definitions are to provide politics with a distinctive identity:

> If politics consists, as Leftwich says, of *all* the activities of cooperation and conflict in the production and reproduction of social life, what does it exclude? Politics ceases to be just one 'aspect' of a human association ... and becomes merely another word for human activity itself.[30]

This criticism is apt. Although Leftwich is strongly opposed to the specialised division of labour in the social sciences (which he argues obscures our understanding of societies and their problems),[31] he advocates an *inter*disciplinary approach, not a merging of all disciplines into one, but his definition makes it obscure how politics could leave any aspect of social activity unclaimed.

(From Andrew Mason, 'Politics and the state', *Political Studies*, XXXVIII, 1990, pp. 575–587.)

Occasionally, even longer quotations may be desirable. In such cases, you should be careful to preserve the paragraphing of the original.

It is essential to acknowledge any material quoted directly or indirectly. Be careful to use borrowed material sparingly and selectively. The indiscriminate use of quotations is as bad as a lack of them. You will certainly not make a good impression by submitting work which is full of quotations.

FOOTNOTES

Footnotes are used to provide additional explanations or details of work by other writers referred to in the main text. They are generally indicated by a raised number at the end of the sentence to which reference is made. Look at the three examples, numbered 29–31, in the text in the short task above.

There are two generally accepted systems of footnotes. They may appear at the bottom of the page to which they refer, in which case they are usually separated from the main text by a ruled line. Alternatively, they may be found at the end of a piece of work (in a book, this could be the end of a chapter or the end of the book). Normally, such information placed at the end of work is given the heading 'Notes'. You should consult your department to find out which convention is preferred.

Look at the following example from the bottom of the page of a text:

Fernando Pessoa sought to resolve the tensions in his personality by breaking his poetic self down into four different authors.[1] In adopting such a path, he was clearly echoing Keats's famous observation that 'the poetic character ... is not itself – it has no self ... A poet is the most unpoetical of anything in existence; because he has no Identity – he is continually informing and filling some other Body...'.[2]

[1] Each of these four authors wrote in a way which the other three were unable or not permitted to.
[2] John Keats, 'A Letter to Richard Woodhouse', 27th October 1818, in *The Letters of John Keats* (ed. H. Buxton Forman), London: Reeves and Turner, 1895.

In the above example, the two footnotes relating to the text on the same page are placed at the foot of the page. They could equally well be placed at the end of the chapter or whole piece of work in a section entitled 'Notes'. More recently published material tends to favour the latter convention. It is particularly desirable if there is a large amount of additional material.

DIVIDING A TEXT INTO PARAGRAPHS

The amount of information contained in one paragraph may differ depending on what you are writing and the culture in which you are writing. In some types of writing, paragraphs may consist of one or two sentences. Although you may have noticed short paragraphs in newspaper articles which are written in English, they are *not* common in academic writing.

In academic English, paragraph writing often tends to observe the conventions listed below. While many writers may not follow these conventions, they are useful for you to follow, especially if you have trouble organising your writing. It is always worth trying to visualise how easily a reader will be able to follow your writing, and these conventions are designed to facilitate reading.

(a) A paragraph should usually deal with one main topic.

(b) The main topic may be expressed in a topic sentence. This is a sentence which expresses the central idea of a paragraph and serves to unify its content. The topic sentence is often (but not always) the first sentence in a paragraph. This position helps the reader follow the ideas presented in an orderly fashion.

(c) The idea expressed is developed from one sentence to the next by sentences which add information closely related to the topic sentence.

(d) A new main topic should be dealt with in a new paragraph.

Short task

Study the following paragraph and notice how the ideas are developed.

(1) The fantastic water clarity of the Mount Gambier sinkholes results from several factors. (2) The holes are fed from aquifers holding rainwater that fell decades – even centuries – ago, and that has been filtered through miles of limestone. (3) The high level of calcium that limestone adds causes the silty detritus from dead plants and animals to cling together and settle quickly to the bottom. (4) Abundant bottom vegetation in the shallow sinkholes also helps bind the silt. (5) And the rapid turnover of water prohibits stagnation.

(From H. Hauser, 'Exploring a sunken realm in Australia', *National Geographic*, vol. 165, no.1, 1984.)

The paragraph above consists of five sentences. Sentence 1 is the topic sentence. Sentences 2–5 all serve to develop the idea; in this case by giving reasons for the clarity of the water.

When writing an essay, it is worth checking that you have divided it into paragraphs and that the paragraphs follow the conventions described above.

Short task

Look at the division of paragraphs and development of ideas in each paragraph in the long extract below.

Sex-differences

That there are differences between the sexes is hardly a matter of dispute. On the average, females have more fat and less muscle than males, are not as strong, and weigh less. They also mature more rapidly and live longer. The female voice has different characteristics from the male voice, and often females and males exhibit different ranges of verbal skills.

But we must also be aware that social factors may account for some of the difference. For example, women may live longer than men because of the different roles they play in society and the different jobs they tend to fill. Differences in voice quality may be accentuated by beliefs about what men and women *should* sound like when they talk, and any differences in verbal skills are undoubtedly explained in great part through differences in upbringing. (It has often been noted that there is far more reading failure in schools among boys than girls, but it does not follow from this fact that boys are inherently less well equipped to learn to read, for their poor performance in comparison to girls may be socio-cultural in origin rather than genetic.)

Numerous observers have described women's speech as being different from that of men. In the linguistic literature perhaps the most famous example of linguistic differentiation between the sexes is said to occur in the lesser Antilles of the West Indies among the Carib Indians. Male and female

Caribs are said to speak different languages, the result of a long-ago conquest in which a group of invading Carib-speaking men killed the local Arawak-speaking men and mated with the Arawak women. The descendants of these Carib-speaking men and Arawak-speaking women are sometimes described as having different languages for men and women. There are, for example, differences in the genders ascribed to abstract nouns, with these treated grammatically as feminine by males and masculine by females. The differences actually do not result in two 'separate' or 'different' languages, but rather one language with noticeable sex-based characteristics (Taylor, 1951b). Further investigations of other languages show us that these kinds of differences between men and women are really quite widespread. The interesting question is why this should be so.

Phonological differences between the speech of men and women have been noted in a variety of languages. In a northeast Asian language, Yukaghir, both women and children have /ts/ and /dz/ where men have /tj/ and /dj/. Old people of *both* sexes have a corresponding /cj/ and /jj/. Therefore, the difference is not only sex-related but also age-graded. Consequently, in his lifetime a male goes through the progression of /ts/, /tj/, and /cj/, and /dz/, /dj/ and /jj/, and a female has a corresponding /ts/ and /cj/ and /dz and /jj/. In Bengali, men often substitute /l/ for

initial /n/; women, children, and the uneducated do not do this. Likewise, in a Siberian language, Chuckchi, men, but not women, often drop /n/ and /t/ when they occur between vowels, e.g., female 'nitva-quenat' and male 'nitvaqaat'. In Montreal many more men than women do not pronounce the /l/ in the pronouns and articles 'il', 'elle', 'la' and 'les'. Schoolgirls in Scotland apparently pronounce the /t/ in words like 'water' and 'got' more often than schoolboys, who prefer to substitute a glottal stop.

In the area of morphology and vocabulary, many of the studies have focused on English. Lakoff (1973), for example, claims that women use color words like 'mauve', 'beige', 'aquamarine', 'lavender', and 'magenta' but most men do not. She also maintains that adjectives such as 'adorable', 'charming', 'divine', 'lovely', and 'sweet' are also commonly used by women but only very rarely by men. However, we have no empirical evidence that such is actually the case. Women are also said to have their own vocabulary for emphasising certain effects on them, words and expressions such as 'so good', 'such fun', 'exquisite', 'lovely', 'divine', 'precious', 'adorable', 'darling', and 'fantastic'. Furthermore, English as a language, is said to make certain distinctions of a sex-based kind, e.g., 'actor – actress', 'waiter – waitress', and 'master – mistress'.

(From Ronald Wardhaugh, *An Introduction to Sociolinguistics*, Blackwell, 1986. Reproduced by permission of Blackwell.)

WRITING INTRODUCTIONS AND CONCLUSIONS

The main parts of an essay are:

1. the introduction
2. the body
3. the conclusion.

1. THE INTRODUCTION

As its name implies, the introductory paragraph or section should provide a clear introduction to the content of your essay. It should introduce the central idea or main purpose of your writing. A good introductory paragraph or section will serve as a focus and stimulus to your readers, encouraging them to continue reading.

You should make sure the length of the introduction is in proportion to the rest of the essay; the length may range from a single paragraph to a complete section in itself. An examination answer may not require an introduction at all. The level of formality of the language should be appropriate to academic work and the style of language should reflect that of the rest of the essay.

Extended pieces of academic writing (i.e. dissertations or theses) and, in many cases, academic journal articles, will be preceded by an *abstract*, which is a brief summary of the whole text and not an introduction. Below is an example from a journal article in which a brief abstract (in bold type) is followed by the introduction.

Are we responsible for our actions? If we follow the assumptions on which the classical mechanistic–reductionist paradigm is based to their logical conclusion, we appear to be led to the conclusion that we are not masters of our destiny or ultimately responsible for our moral decisions. But recent developments in science are undermining this reply.

Have the human sciences removed from us all responsibility for the things we do? Can we be blamed for our actions? If we follow the assumptions on which the classical mechanistic–reductionist paradigm is based to their logical conclusion, we are led to believe that we are not masters of our destiny or ultimately responsible for our moral decisions. The first part of this article aims to explain why this is so before we turn to more recent developments in science to see how these assumptions have been undermined and this classical world view opened to question.

(From Philip Bligh, 'The implications of reductionist physics for human culpability', *Physics Education* 24, 1989.)

2. THE BODY

Key ideas and issues presented in the introduction should be developed in the main body of the essay in a logical and coherent manner. The purpose of your essay must be clear and the reader must be able to follow its development without any problems. The relationship between parts of the writing should be easily recognisable. Main points should be presented in separate paragraphs and should be pertinent to the main purpose of the essay.

Main ideas and arguments should be presented clearly and support for these ideas should be provided. In an academic essay or paper, the main ideas and supporting arguments are often positioned immediately after the introduction.

3. THE CONCLUSION

The conclusion should signal to your readers that you have finished your writing and should leave them with the clear impression that the purposes of the essay have been achieved. The most common types of conclusion may include:

a) A summary of the main points.

b) Concluding statements drawn from the points made in the main body.

c) Recommendations of action to be taken.

SYNTHESISING INFORMATION FROM MORE THAN ONE SOURCE

In addition to summarising individual texts, and incorporating references and quotations from them, you will probably often have to synthesise information from two or more sources. This may be done in several ways and for several purposes. For example, synthesis may involve:

- a simple presentation of differing or supporting (view)points.
- a presentation of (view)points with additional comment by you.
- (view)points incorporated into your work which you may challenge or support, or use as a basis for your own ideas.

Below are two examples of synthesising from more than one source.

> The most consistent research over a period of twenty-five years has been undertaken in Canada by Gardner and Lambert at McGill University (Gardner and Lambert, 1972) and later by Gardner and his colleagues at the University of Western Ontario in London, Ontario (for example, Gardner, 1979; Gardner and Smythe, 1981). These studies have focused on learners' social attitudes, values, and the motivation of learners in relation to other learner factors and the learning outcome.

(From H. H. Stern, *Fundamental Concepts of Language Teaching*. Oxford University Press, 1983.)

> In another article in *ELT Journal*, Allwright discusses the need for teachers to adopt 'more of a research attitude to their ordinary lives as teachers' (1983:132), and Brumfit (1984) devotes an entire book to the exploration and evolution of a teacher's conceptual framework for integrating research and theory with teaching. Theory is therefore seen as playing a central role in the practice of teaching.

(From E. Ramani, 'Theorizing from the classroom', *ELT Journal*, vol. 41, no. 1, 1987.)

In the first example, there is a simple presentation of supporting information. In the second example, two supporting viewpoints are given in the first sentence to support the writer's idea in the second.

COMPARISON AND CONTRAST

Often you will need to compare and contrast two or more items of fact, ideas or viewpoints in an essay. It is assumed that there are basic similarities between what is being compared or contrasted; otherwise, there would be no basis for doing either.

There are two main ways in which essays of comparison and contrast can be organised:

1. Take all the main points concerning one subject, or information from one source, and present them in one paragraph. Follow by another paragraph presenting all the main points concerning the second subject or source. This can be described as a 'vertical' arrangement. For example:

   Paragraph 1 – Source/Subject A: Point 1
                                                   Point 2
                                                   Point 3

   Paragraph 2 – Source/Subject B: Point 1
                                                   Point 2
                                                   Point 3

2. Take each point in turn and contrast them immediately, point by point. This can be described as a 'horizontal' arrangement. For example:

Source/Subject A		Source/Subject B
Point 1	$\rightarrow$	Point 1
Point 2	$\rightarrow$	Point 2
Point 3	$\rightarrow$	Point 3

The second method may be better when the topic is longer and more complex. In this case, you will also need to consider the question of paragraphing, each paragraph dealing only with one main point and connected subsidiary points.

In addition to choosing one of the two methods of comparison and contrast described above, a third option is to consider a combination of both the vertical pattern (1) and the horizontal pattern (2). This is useful in extended writing, but it requires very careful paragraph arrangement.

The Writing book in this series gives extensive practice in writing essays of comparison and contrast.

UNIT 3

WRITING SKILLS: TASKS

TASK 1

Read the following text and then see how parts of it have been incorporated in different ways into students' work in 1–4 below.

Environmental refugees

Degradation of soil, deforestation and desertification have during the 1980s created a new class of displaced people: environmental refugees. Growing human pressure has triggered off a self-reinforcing process of ecological deterioration, and more people are being affected by natural catastrophes. The protracted drought in sub-Saharan Africa forced at least 2 million persons in some sub-Saharan and East African countries to abandon their traditional areas in the early 1980s, and as many as 10 million in the mid-1980s. Presently the total population of these countries is some 80 million, but by the year 2025 sub-Saharan Africa will be the home of a probable 200 million people. As things look now, ecological disasters will force a large proportion of the people in these and neighbouring countries to abandon their homes again and again.

Lack of water increasingly forces people onto the move: 1.7 billion people, spread among 80 countries, are already suffering serious water shortage. But so too does superabundance of water. Deforestation of upland watersheds is the main factor behind the growing severity of floods like the one which ravaged Bangladesh in 1988 leaving 25 million homeless. Deforestation in the South, together with industrial pollution in the North, is a major factor behind global warming, which within 40–70 years may cause the flooding of important coastal areas. Rises of 7–67 centimetres are predicted by the middle of the next century. In Bangladesh, a one-metre sea-level rise by the year 2025 would displace some 20–25 million people. Bangladesh, currently with 116 million inhabitants, already has a population density on its available land more than twice as high as the Netherlands. Towards the end of the next century it might host 325 million inhabitants. Many of them will have no choice but to move elsewhere before they are taken away by the floods.

(From Jonas Widgren 'International migration and regional stability', *International Affairs*, vol. 66, no. 4, 1990, p. 759.)

The incorporations of information from the above text which are given below are all acceptable and have been acknowledged. However, the *form* of the acknowledgement is not always acceptable. Which of the following incorporations are acknowledged in an acceptable way?

1. As Widgren (1990: 759) has pointed out, a new class of displaced person (environmental refugees) emerged in the 1980s as a result of soil degradation, desertification and deforestation.

2. Both lack of water and superabundance of water have contributed to the growing number of environmental refugees in the world (Widgren, 1990).

3. In the article 'International migration and regional stability (*International Affairs*, 66, 4, 1990, p. 759), Jonas Widgren distinguishes a rapidly growing new class of displaced people, namely environmental refugees.

4. Widgren (1990: 759) points out that while lack of water may be one reason forcing people to move, an excess of water may also be responsible, with 'deforestation of upland watersheds ... the main factor behind the growing severity of floods like the one which ravaged Bangladesh in 1988 leaving 25 million homeless'.

TASK 2

Look at the text below. Consider the ways in which the essay extracts that follow have incorporated information from it. Which are acceptable?

A *New Scientist* survey in 1982 concluded that 'the attitude of the non-scientific general public stems from a lack of understanding of what science is, and what scientists do' (Ferry and Moore, 1982). This is in accord with the ideas expressed by C.P. Snow (1964) when he spoke of 'the gulf of mutual incomprehension' that lies between the literary and scientific worlds, which manifests itself as 'hostility and dislike, but most of all, a lack of understanding'.

Research on the student view of 'the scientist' began in the USA with Meade and Metraux (1957) making a pilot study on 'The image of the scientist among high school students'. Many of the students in their sample visualised a scientist as a rather eccentric bespectacled man who wears a white coat and works in a laboratory containing a lot of glassware. The authors suggested that the students' attitudes may reflect both the influence of the mass media and also their parents' ideas: these arise in a general 'climate of opinion' extending to the views held by the bureaucracy.

(From Janice Emens McAdam, 'The persistent stereotype: children's images of the scientist', *Physics Education*, vol. 25, 1990, pp. 102–5.)

Extract 1

McAdam (1990: 102) mentions a *New Scientist* survey which came to the conclusion that "the attitude of the non-scientific general public stems from a lack of understanding of what science is, and what scientists do" (Ferry and Moore, 1982). Moreover, she points out that the above conclusion is 'in accord with the ideas expressed by C. P. Snow (1964) when he spoke of the "gulf of mutual incomprehension" that lies between literary and scientific worlds…' This gulf, claimed Snow, revealed itself as "hostility and dislike, but most of all, lack of understanding".

Extract 2

A *New Scientist* survey (Ferry, G. and Moore, J., 'True confessions of women in science', *New Scientist*, 1 July, 1982, pp. 27–30) is mentioned by Janice Emens McAdam in her article 'The persistent stereotype: children's images of scientists' (full details given below). In this survey, Ferry and Moore concluded that 'the attitude of the non-scientific general public stems from a lack of understanding of what science is, and what scientists do'. This is in accord with C. P. Snow in his *The Two Cultures* (New York: Mentor, 1964) when he spoke of the gulf of mutual incomprehension that lies between literary and scientific worlds, which manifests itself as hostility and dislike, but most of all, lack of understanding.

Extract 3

McAdam, describing the work of Meade and Metraux (1957) who carried out a pilot study on 'The image of the scientist among high school students', states that:

> Many of the students in their sample visualised a scientist as a rather eccentric bespectacled man who wears a white coat and works in a laboratory containing a lot of glassware. The authors suggested that the students' attitudes may reflect both the influence of the mass media and also their parents' ideas: these arise in a general 'climate of opinion' extending to the views held by the bureaucracy.[1]

Extract 4

McAdam (6) cites several other studies to support her view of the persistence of children's images of scientists (3, 7, 9).

In Extract 3 above, what does the number at the end of the long quotation signify?

Task 3

In this task you are asked to incorporate quotations in a suitable position in texts.

1. Read the following short text.

> There are many languages in which numerals do not exceed two or three. It may be that those people who use these languages, like the Eskimos, have no great need to use higher numbers. They may be able to give a name to everything in their life without counting. The absence of higher numerals in the language does not imply an inability to adapt to the use of them if the need arises.

Now consider the observation below made by Franz Boas in the *Handbook of American Indian Languages*, published in 1911 by the Smithsonian Institution in Washington DC.

(a) Decide where you could incorporate this observation as a quotation in a suitable place in the above text.

(b) Make any changes necessary in the above text and insert the quotation correctly.

> **It must be borne in mind that counting does not become necessary until objects are considered in such generalized form that their individualities are entirely lost sight of.**

2. Read the following text.

> Britain was the first country to experience an Industrial Revolution. The period of transition from a rural to an industrialised society was a long one. It could, therefore, be argued that change was achieved with comparatively less cost in human terms than in societies which began to industrialise later. However, the notion that the transition in Britain automatically represented an improvement in quality of life for large numbers of people is far from accurate. Britain's experience has been repeated in many other societies that embarked on the path to industrialisation. In some cases, this path was undertaken much more drastically.

Now consider the extract below describing the consequences of industrialisation in Britain, taken from an article entitled 'Cities as if only capital matters' by John Short (1989) which appeared in *The Humane City* (Oxford: Blackwell).

(a) Decide where you could insert this extract as a quotation in the above text.
(b) Rewrite the text, inserting the quotation in an acceptable way.

> **The countryside may have been bleak for the labouring classes but the cities were no better. The Industrial Revolution created cities dominated by private greed often at the expense of broader social values, community concerns and human dignity.**

3. Read the following text.

> More than half a century before Einstein was born, the botanist Robert Brown
> observed through his microscope the behaviour of fine particles of pollen
> suspended on the surface of water. He noticed that they were not stationary but
> in a state of continuous random motion. This phenomenon led him to conclude
> that the particles had a property of their own since it seemed that the movement
> was not caused either by currents in the fluid or its evaporation. In recent years,
> it has been claimed that Brown did not sufficiently safeguard his observations to
> prevent the influence of these external factors (Deutsch, 1991) and his methods
> have been re-examined and defended (Cadee and Ford, 1992). Brown's
> conclusion that living and non-living matter were both made up of the same
> 'primitive molecules' is certainly one that continues to lie at the heart of
> discussions on the meaning of life.
>
> For nearly eighty years, the phenomenon of 'Brownian motion' became a focus
> of attention for physicists and chemists who sought to find a better explanation
> of what happened. For example, Exner (1867) found that the smallest particles
> had the most rapid movement which was increased by light and heat rays, while
> Jevons (1870) postulated that electrical forces caused the phenomenon. The
> latter idea was disproved by Dancer (1870).
>
> It was not until a series of papers by Einstein dating from 1905 that the debate
> came to a conclusion. Einstein's findings were based on exact calculations and
> he was not even sure that what he had discovered corresponded to accounts of
> 'Brownian motion'. He was also unaware of the most precise investigations of
> the phenomenon that had been made before, namely those of Gouy (1888).

Consider the extract below. It is taken from the introduction to the first of the
series of papers by Einstein mentioned in the above text. It appeared in
Investigations on the Theory of the Brownian Movement by Albert Einstein, ed. R.
Furth, published in London by Methuen in 1926.

(a) Decide where you could insert the extract in the above text. You may decide
to insert it either in partial or in complete form.

(b) Rewrite the paragraph in which you have decided to make the insertion,
making any necessary changes in order to insert the quotation.

> **In this paper it will be shown that according to the molecular–kinetic theory of heat,
> bodies of microscopically visible size suspended in a liquid will perform movements
> of such magnitude that they can easily be observed in a microscope, on account of
> the molecular motions of heat.**

TASK 4

Read the following example, which is a combination of reporting and direct
quotation.

> As Stern (1987) has noted, it was for a long time commonly believed that children's intellectual development was negatively affected by using two languages rather than one. This prevailing view only began to change after 1962 when 'a study by Peal and Lambert … claimed that bilingualism was not necessarily a disadvantage and could in fact be beneficial to the individual' (Stern, 1987: 295).

(a) Now use a similar combination of reporting and direct quotation to describe what the writer of the text below says about:

(i)   how serious the destruction of cultural property is
(ii) what the most common cause of damage is.

Cultural property is the term used by the United Nations to denote sites of archaeological (prehistoric), palaeontological, historical, religious, and unique natural value. The ability of today's generation to destroy cultural property is without precedent. Exponential population growth, coupled with powerful technologies and industrialisation, is causing a serious cultural crisis, akin to the crisis of vanishing and endangered species. Around the world, irreplaceable cultural sites are damaged daily. With every destroyed site, future generations lose an opportunity to be enriched by their cultural history.

The conservation of cultural property cannot always be given absolute priority, but much current destruction is unnecessary. With careful planning and cooperation, economic progress need not be at odds with the preservation of cultural heritage. Indeed, it can be forcefully argued that the preservation of cultural property is beneficial and necessary to progress.

Ironically, the most common source of damage and loss is the construction of large public works designed to improve the quality of life. These include dams and reservoirs, large irrigation systems or other agricultural works, and transport corridors (highways, airports, railroads). Other important causes are drilling, mining and urban development. Many of these large-scale development projects are financed and planned with the help of the international development community. Thus, the agencies and institutions that finance and execute projects must consider the issues and values associated with cultural property. To give these issues proper cognizance, agencies must acquire the necessary technical, legal and institutional information. Most bilateral and multilateral development agencies have yet to do so.

Most developing countries, for their part, have a voluminous body of national legislation for preserving cultural property, but they lack the well-defined policies and procedures, as well as the institutional capacity, needed to put the laws into effective action. Plans for new developments are often allowed to proceed to the point of no return before the likely effects on cultural property are considered.

(From Robert Goodland, 'Management of cultural property in bank projects', *Finance and Development*, March 1988.)

(b) Read the following text and then report:

    (i) the similarity in the motivation of both scientists and artists

    (ii) the dissimilarity in society's expectations of their activities.

What motivates a scientist is the burning desire to find out. There is the excitement and fascination of the chase and the unutterable joy at discovery. I have hardly the words to express the thrill, the wonder, when Dr Pan Kiang in Peking pushed a fossil across his desk for me to look at. It was the most wonderful object I had ever seen. It was a naturally formed replica in iron of the blood vessels, nerves, brains and inner ear of one of the earliest backboned animals that lived on earth some 400 million years ago. To see what looked like a perfect dissection of the soft anatomy of such a long extinct organism – something one would never have imagined possible – was such a devastating emotional event. Such fossils as this are truly as John Fowles describes them 'the poetry of evolution'.

For the past 25 years I have been studying the microscopic structure of the original tissues that came to make up our skeletons and teeth. There have been two mutually exclusive interpretations, one championed by me, and the other mainly by experts in Sweden and the USA. For several years there had been no movement, we had reached an impasse. Then, quite suddenly, I realised we had been asking the wrong questions. The whole confrontational exercise over a quarter of a century had been a complete waste of time. Recounting the details of this seems to upset some scientists but they don't understand the satisfaction of having resolved the controversy. Science is about inner satisfaction and there is not a great deal to choose in emotional terms between scientists and artists. Artists are not expected to account for themselves in the way scientists are. The activities of artists are recognised as an essential part of civilisation but the search for knowledge seems to be only appreciated if a direct commodity emerges from the scientists' endeavours.

(From Beverly Halstead 'A burning passion for knowledge', *The Independent*, 9.11.87.)

Task 5

Divide the following text into paragraphs and be prepared to justify the reasons for your divisions.

The global steel industry changed rapidly over the past decade. Industrial country production declined, while developing countries, as a group, showed rapid increases both in production and as a proportion of world output. Meanwhile, the emergence of new production systems – in the form of 'minimills' (producing 500,000 to 1 million tons a year from scrap steel instead of iron ore) – and new technology has helped change the economics of steel production, altering patterns of international trade and opening the way for further changes in the manufacture of steel. Today, smaller mills serving modest-sized markets have become economic, making it possible for many developing countries that had hitherto steered clear of producing their own steel to enter production. While developing countries would appear to have gained from the new technology and production systems, the steel market in industrial countries has changed too, making it more difficult for new entrants to benefit from export-led growth of the steel sector. This market is moving to just-in-time (i.e. quick response) methods to meet demand. This places a higher premium on keeping mills in close proximity to customers. Moreover, transportation of raw materials now paradoxically costs less than shipments of finished steel goods. Even though world production of steel has been stagnant for the past ten years or so, at around 750 million tons a year, developing countries have shown rapid growth of output. Their share has increased from 7 per cent of world production in 1979 to 12 per cent in 1988. Brazil, China, the Republic of Korea and Turkey have continued to expand their production and now have plans to increase their capacity. Industrial countries, meanwhile, are experiencing a secular decline in steel production. International trade in steel has also shown little growth in the last ten years, in part because of trade constraints, but the pattern of trade has been changing. The European Community and Japan, although still net exporters, have declined in importance. The United States, long a major net importer, has been importing less in the latter half of the 1980s, even though trade restrictions there have not been binding. Brazil has helped increase total Latin American exports, although the region now is a large net exporter of steel. Similarly, Korea continued to increase its exports, but Asia is a net importer.

(From Robert R. Miller, 'The changing economics of steel', *Finance and Development*, June 1991.)

TASK 6

In the text below, the paragraphs are not in the correct order. Rearrange the paragraphs into what you consider to be a suitably coherent order.

Politics of music takes centre stage

Grove (whose *Dictionary of Music and Musicians* is now in its sixth edition) found acolytes such as Elgar, Delius, Vaughan-Williams, Parry and others who created a new 'culture', which in effect repudiated anything later than Purcell – nothing composed in England after 1700 was considered worth listening to.

The research stems from essays they both submitted in 1984 to the Norris paperback, *Music and the Politics of Culture*. The book sold out and is being republished. The grant will enable Hughes to take a year's sabbatical.

Dr. Stradling argues that the conventional emphasis in researching music history is to concentrate on the musical notes, or the biography. Stradling and Hughes' ambition has been to move the discussion towards the culture, politics and social history of the composition.

An unprecedented £25,000 grant has been awarded by the Leverhulme Trust for research into the politics of modern English music. The award will go to Dr. Robert Stradling, lecturer in Spanish history at Cardiff University, and his former student, Meirion Hughes, now a lecturer in 20th-century international politics at Uxbridge College of Further Education.

The period chosen has potent nationalistic overtones. The protagonist was George Grove, Victorian engineer, renaissance man and polymath, involved in the 1851 exhibition and determined to found a movement to match an established strong European musical culture.

Among the papers in the British Manuscript Collection, where Hughes spends most of his research time, is the evidence of another kind of discrimination. England's only working class composer, Havergal Brian, who lived from 1876 to 1972, in council houses in Reading and Harrow, was also one of the country's most prolific. He composed more than 40 symphonies, and his Gothic Symphony is the largest known in terms of forces needed and performance time. Yet in what was almost an aristocratic field he remained virtually ignored.

Following the success of the Norris paperback, Stradling asked the Leverhulme Trust to back specific research into the period 1871 to 1940 – a period coinciding with the English Musical Revival. He got crucial support from Professor Alexander Goehr of Cambridge and emeritus Professor Wilfred Mellers of York – the two most eminent living musicologists and historians of music.

(From 'Politics of music take centre stage', *The Times Higher Educational Supplement*, 12.4.91.)

TASK 7

Look at the four introductions on the following pages, taken from articles in academic journals. Then look at the list of features below. Which of those features can you identify in one or more of the introductions? (**Note**: Do not worry about the specialised content of the writing but consider, in general terms, the kind of information that introductions give and look for language that conveys such information.)

1. a statement of the importance of the subject (e.g. the degree of attention that has recently been given to it, the seriousness of a problem)
2. mention of previous (recent) work on the subject or of the absence of such work
3. justification for dealing with the subject
4. a statement of the writer's objective in the present work
5. a statement of limitations to the scope of the present work
6. brief details of different parts of the main body of the work
7. mention of differing viewpoints on the subject
8. the writer's viewpoint
9. mention of future research on the subject
10. a definition

1.

INTRODUCTION

During the past quarter-century, research on hillslope runoff and erosion processes has proceeded rapidly in humid landscapes (e.g., KIRKBY, 1978; WISCHMEIER & SMITH, 1978; FOSTER, 1982), but fewer studies have been undertaken in desert environments and progress has been slower (e.g. EMMETT, 1970; YAIR & KLEIN, 1973; YAIR & LAVEE, 1976, 1977; YAIR et al, 1980; IVERSON, 1980; SIMANTON & RENARD, 1982; SIMANTON et al, 1984; ABRAHAMS et al, 1986). Moreover, most studies in desert environments have been conducted in only a handful of areas (e.g., the Negev, Sinai Peninsula, and Walnut Gulch), too few to provide a good understanding of the variability and controls of hillslope runoff and erosion processes in deserts in general. Consequently, there is a pressing need for additional studies to both broaden and deepen our knowledge of these processes in desert landscapes.

In this paper we report on an investigation of the hydrologic and sediment responses of desert hillslopes in Walnut Gulch

Experimental Watershed, southern Arizona. Hillslope responses in this watershed have already been examined in some detail by the Agricultural Research Service (e.g., TROMBLE, 1976; SIMANTON & RENARD, 1982; SIMANTON et al, 1984). However, this body of research has been confined to standard USLE plots, which have gradients of 9° (5.14). Thus, a principal objective of the present study was to extend this research to steeper slopes. This was done by applying simulated rainfall to runoff plots ranging in gradient up to 33° and analysing

(1) temporal variations in surface runoff and sediment concentration during a single rainstorm on each plot, and

(2) spatial variations in runoff characteristics and sediment yield among the plots.

These analyses afford a number of insights into hillslope runoff and erosion processes at Walnut Gulch and permit some useful comparisons with other desert landscapes.

(FROM: A. D. Abrahams, A. J. Parsons and Shiu-hung Luk, 'Hydrologic and sediment responses to simulated rainfall on desert hillslopes in Southern Arizona', *Catena*, vol. 15, pp. 103–117.)

2.

INTRODUCTION

In recent years 'scientific' or 'critical' realism, along with various forms of 'antirealism', have become topics of lively debate. The literature makes good reading – authors from a variety of fields displaying skill in argument and employing interesting illustrations from the history of science. My plan here is to highlight one feature of this debate and then to explain it in a way that I hope will shed fresh light on the entire issue. That feature is the *lack of convergence* in the discussion. There are numerous positions on both sides. 'Scientific realism,' says Jarrett Leplin, 'is a majority position whose advocates are so divided as to appear a minority' ([1984], p. 1). There are even more radical divi-

sions among the realists' opponents; each attempt at classification of the antirealists produces different results. For that matter, it is not entirely clear who is on which side. Arthur Fine lists supporters of his own 'nonrealist' position that include both avowed realists and antirealists ([1984], pp. 102–3). The status of the realist thesis is subject to debate. Is it a metaphysical claim descendant from earlier denials of idealism? Is it an empirical hypothesis supported by its ability to account for the success of science? Is it a tautology? Finally (and this is most significant for my thesis), participants in the discussion claim not to understand one another.

My diagnosis of this lack of convergence – one might even say, confusion – is the following: Sometime just after the middle of this century a revolution took place in philosophy – a 'paradigm shift' – that represents so radical a change in conceptions of knowledge and language that inhabitants of the old and new philosophical worlds often talk past one another. It is too soon to be sure, but I think it likely that further historians will see this turn of events to be equally as important as the turn from medieval to modern philosophy. Perhaps it is not premature to desig-

nate the new philosophy as 'postmodern' (despite the fact that deconstructionists have already found their own use for this term).

In the following pages I shall propose a scheme for distinguishing between modern and postmodern philosophy, and then suggest that there are both modern and postmodern versions of realism and antirealism – hence the confusion, the inability to be quite sure what one is arguing *against*.

Nancey Murphy, 'Scientific realism and postmodern philosophy', *British Journal for the Philosophy of Science*, vol. 41, 1990, pp. 291–303.

3.

INTRODUCTION

The analysis of injury in intellectual property cases filed with the US International Trade Commission (ITC) under Section 337 of the Tariff Act of 1930 has become more controversial in recent years, as the more general trade problems of the United States have caused increasing attention to be focused on imports resulting from 'unfair trade practices'. This article will concentrate on the economic arguments behind Commission views on this question since the Trade Act of 1974.[1] Given the possibility that the injury requirement will be removed for intellectual property infringements in the current session of Congress (their deletion having been put forward, for the second consecutive session, in a bill passing the US House of Representatives), my comments may turn out to be retrospective on this issue. While some reference will be made to the international legal and political environment in which the ITC operates, detailed discussion of the broader trade context is beyond the scope of the work presented here.

Before continuing, consider the word-

ing of Section 337(a) of the Tariff Act of 1930 as amended:[2]

"Unfair methods of competition and unfair acts in the importation of articles into the United States, or in their sale by the owner, importer, consignee, or agent of either, the effect or tendency of which is to destroy or substantially injure an industry, efficiently and economically operated, in the United States, or to prevent the establishment of such an industry, or to restrain or monopolize trade and commerce in the United States, are declared unlawful and when found by the Commission to exist shall be dealt with, in addition to any other provision of law, as provided in this section."

After a brief discussion of the economics of intellectual property rights (and of their infringement) in the next section, an overview of ITC enforcement in this area will be given in section III. This will be followed by a discussion of industry definition in section IV, and an analysis of the injury issue in section V. The final section will present some conclusions.

Robert M. Feinberg, 'Intellectual property, injury, and international trade', *Journal of World Trade*, vol. 22, no. 2, 1988.

4.

INTRODUCTION

The processes of economic restructuring in the United Kingdom have been thoroughly researched over recent years.[1] It has become well established that the decline in employment has been greatest in the traditional, manufacturing industries and hence concentrated in the industrial locations: the north of England and the central belt of Scotland.[2] Strathclyde Region is typical of areas that have done badly. Traditional employment bases of shipbuilding, steel, coal and engineering have been in long-term decline and, because the region is geographically peripheral to the boom areas in the south-east of England, it has not benefited greatly from the new growing employment sectors. As part of the strategy for increasing economic prosperity in the region, the Scottish Development Agency attempts to attract businesses into the area. Policy aims include attracting and fostering new businesses as well as trying to attract relocating branches or divisions of national and multinational firms.

The key question that this article will address is the extent to which housing policy should be incorporated into this process. Most planning authorities would probably want to consider the consequences of their plans on the likelihood of attracting new employment into the area and would attempt to take into account demands from in-movers when planning land release for new house building. However, there is seldom a readily available information base from which to estimate the extent of these demands or to judge the wider effects of housing plans. Rather, planners are likely to receive a mass of contradictory evidence, from the building industry, from exchange professionals in housing (building societies, sol-

icitors, estate agents), from local pressure groups and from the evidence of their own projections. They then face the difficult task of trying to reconcile these different viewpoints and must reach a compromise, which is unlikely to satisfy everyone. Provision for executive in-movers has been a controversial issue in Strathclyde.[3]

This article will report on work that was undertaken in order to investigate, first, the housing market impacts of in-movers and, second, the extent to which the housing market satisfied the demands from these in-movers.[4] The work aimed to analyse both the extent to which the housing market was responding adequately to the demands from in-movers and the extent to which the planning system was making adequate allowances for the preferences of in-movers in its structure plan.[5] The method adopted here is suggested as a way in which some key issues may be objectively gauged and hence might assist in reaching more rational planning decisions in the face of conflicting pressures.

The article has six further main sections. The next section briefly outlines the role that executive mobility has in economic regeneration and the relationship between housing and firm location. The third section presents more detail on the Strathclyde context, presenting the key features of the housing market and the planning context. The fourth part presents evidence from an analysis of house price trends in the executive housing market. The fifth section describes the key characteristics of executive house buyers and the sixth analyses the experience of executive movers themselves. The final section presents conclusions and policy implications.

Moira Munro and Peter Symon, 'Planning for Strathclyde's regeneration', *Town Planning Review*, vol. 61, no. 1, 1990.)

TASK 8

Without focusing on content, which you may not understand, look at the following conclusions from articles in academic journals. Which of the features listed below do they contain?

1. a summary of the main body of the text
2. a deduction made on the basis of what has been discussed in the main body
3. the writer's personal opinion of the subject discussed
4. mention of other people's research on the subject
5. a statement of dissatisfaction with gaps or limitations in the work
6. a comment relating to the future (often in the form of a prediction/ projection) which is based on what has been discussed in the main body
7. implications of findings in the main body for policy and/or future research
8. highly important facts or figures not mentioned in the main body

1.

CONCLUSION

It is concluded that stream aggradation was a response to both baselevel controls and high sediment yields exceeding stream capacity. Stream bed aggradation resultant on sediment supply characterised the stream in the upper parts of the basins. While in the distal parts of the streams, stream bed aggradation was controlled by baselevel constraints. An obvious direction concluding discussion could take, is to infer that stream aggradation was diachronous, with baselevel and sediment controls acting at different times. But for the sake of parsimony, and until absolute dates become available, and/or reliable stratigraphic evidence has been obtained, it is assumed that the two processes acted in concert, and that aggradation was penecontemporaneous throughout the small basins.

(From K. H. Wyrwoll, 'Determining the causes of pleistocene stream aggradation in the central coastal areas of Western Australia', *Catena*, vol. 15, pp. 39–51.

2.

CONCLUSION

This paper has provided a systematic study of the integrated approach to deductive DBS design and implementation. The study has been carried out by separating the issue into three levels of coupling: logical, function and physical levels. These levels of coupling deal with, respectively, the expressive power of query languages, the interaction between LIFs and RDMFs, and the physical organisation of deductive databases. The coupling strategies considered here, while they abstract some fundamental and common issues for deductive DBS design and implementation, serve as a useful tool for evaluating many existing deductive DBSs.

It should be noted that in this paper, only the various coupling problems were addressed, and no limitation was assumed as to how sophisticated each component should be. It is possible to extend the functionality of each component in its own right. For example, the LPL at the logical level itself can be extended to support more advanced deduction facilities, such as nonmonotonic reasoning or fuzzy logic.[30] These extensions will possibly enhance the functionality of the resultant deductive DBSs, but they will not affect the generality of the coupling problems discussed here.

Finally, it is worth pointing out that in the longer term, a homogenous deductive DBS is probably preferable to an integrated one. In this type of deductive DBS, the division between logical interference and database manipulation will exist not as *independent components* as shown in Figure 1, but as *functionally dedicated modules* within one system. For example, a uniform collection of logical clauses, such as dictionary clauses, database clauses, deductive laws and integrity constraints, can be used to represent the real world. Current experience is largely confined to integrated deductive DBSs, and these are far away from meeting this objective. The deductive DBSs constructed so far are only trying to provide a deductive view for relational DBSs, so that users can formulate their retrieval problems in terms of logical deduction. It is hoped that developments in the integrated deductive DBSs will eventually lead to pragmatic homogeneous systems. But the take-up of this by users will be greatly enhanced by an evolutionary rather than a revolutionary approach.

From D. A. Bell, J. Shao and M. E. C. Hull, 'Integrative deductive database system implementation: a scientific study', *The Computer Journal*, vol. 33, no. 1, 1990.

3.

CONCLUSION

The effects of noise are widespread – on individual and social functioning, and on performance efficiency. This article has only been able to touch on the most prominent features of its effects. Although we may take comfort from the trend toward rather more careful management of our environment, this argument has usually been cast in terms of lowering the overall level of noise. While this will reduce the risk of hearing impairment, it will do very little to ameliorate the human distress of noise annoyance and a range of detrimental effects on performance. These effects are largely independent of intensity, they have more to do either with the social or political context in which the sound appears or, as is the case with speech, the special status accorded to some sounds by the brain. Even if the world was a much quieter place, the problem of unwanted sound would still be with us.

From Dylan M. Jones, 'Noise, stress and human behaviour', *Environmental Health*, 1990.

4.

CONCLUSION

Even a preliminary study such as the one reported here has highlighted ten potential sources of mismatch between teacher intention and learner interpretation. Clearly, further studies are needed to understand several already determined, and yet undetermined, mismatches that classroom events are capable of generating. For the success of task-based pedagogy, teachers and learners have to function as partners in the joint production of the discourse of lessons in the L2 classroom. It is, therefore, important that we understand contradictory intentions and interpretations of classroom participants if we are serious about facilitating desired learning outcomes in the classroom. A knowledge of potential sources of the mismatch between teacher intention and learner interpretation will help us sensitise ourselves to the exact demands made by language-learning tasks.

Of course, mismatches between teacher intention and learner interpretation may be inevitable, but they need not be totally negative. A particular mismatch, if identified and properly handled, can give learners an opportunity to negotiate further in order to tease out a problem in their own way. In fact, as Candlin (1987: 17) points out, 'it would be ironic if a task-based syllabus merely made learners expert at following pre-set paths and did not promote their own capacities to draw their own maps.' What is needed is an understanding of the learners' capacity to draw their own maps so that we can promote successful learning outcomes. As Breen (1987: 40) observes, 'any task is, by definition, an intervention upon personal approaches to learning and personal concepts of what language learning is like.' The more we know about the learner's personal approaches and personal concepts, the better and more productive our intervention will be.

From B. Kumaravadivelu, 'Teacher intention and learner interpretation', *ELT Journal*, vol. 45, no. 2, April 1991.

TASK 9

On the following pages, you will find eight extracts from four academic journal articles. First establish which are introductions and which are conclusions. Then match each introduction with a conclusion.

1.

This discussion has given an overview of methods of genetic improvement in developing countries, with special interest in the use of nucleus breeding units. There is such a range of species, conditions, requirements and possibilities that only general guidelines can be given. Initially there should be opportunities in selecting the best stocks (either exotic or local) and in their exploitation, for example through crossing systems. For genetic improvement within developing countries, the use of nucleus breeding units is proposed.

Sample selection systems for the main breeding objectives should be developed first and be shown to work. Elaboration of the breeding objective and the use of new technologies or more complex breeding systems to increase rates of genetic change can be developed later. The close involvement of producers and breeders, though they are often conservative, is stressed to keep the breeding schemes relevant to practice and to the livestock industry.

2.

In many of the developed countries following the Second World War, there existed a widespread presumption of the need to expand public spending and accommodate increases in the relative size of the government sector. This was based on the view that greater government intervention was the best, if not the only way to achieve certain economic and social goals. Since the 1970s, however, the validity of this view has been questioned. Not only has there been growing skepticism concerning the possible achievements of public spending, but also increased recognition of the consequent undesirable side effects of financing these expenditures. In particular, the recent emphasis on structural aspects of economic performance has highlighted the risks of creating disincentives to growth that can arise from the government trying to do too much. This, amongst other reasons, has resulted in deliberate policies to curtail the growth in government spending and even to reduce its level.

In the developing countries, meanwhile, the task of organizing the economic structure and promoting faster growth as an explicit goal of economic policy was felt too important to be left to an often nascent private sector. This led to policies of ever-rising public spending often coupled with increased public intervention. The more stringent financial environment following the 1973 and 1979 oil shocks triggered a movement to curtail public expenditure growth in many of these countries.

Underlying the controversy that has often surrounded these policy changes in both developed and developing nations lies an interesting debate concerning the impact on economic growth of cuts in government spending. This article examines the contributions that government expenditure, and in particular the composition of expenditure, can make to the growth process. Such an empirical investigation is important both in assessing the relevance of a widely used growth model and understanding the role of government spending in the growth experience of developing countries. The results could assist policymakers in designing growth-oriented fiscal adjustment programs and setting up expenditure priorities.

3.

"Waste disposal is a $12 billion a year business which annually deals with 300 million tons of toxic waste produced by 24 industrialized countries. It is its scale combined with strong environmental lobby groups in developed countries, and the expense of proper waste management in coded sites that make dumping in the Third World an attractive proposition." (West Africa, 20 June 1988, p. 1108.)

The assessment above captures the central problem of a new and burgeoning issue of economic development in Third World countries, including those in sub-Saharan Africa. Although toxic-waste transfers also occur between industrial countries (French 1988; Potterfield, 1988; British Institution of Water and Environmental Management, 1988), it is different from waste dumping in the Third World in several respects. First, the host government has significant knowledge of the nature of the products; second, the host government has a legal framework in place to control dumping activities; third, the host country possesses the technology to handle the treatment and storage of the waste; and fourth, the host country has the capability to police and limit clandestine dumping. Due to these factors, a First World country makes a decision to host wastes on the basis of informed consent and with a full technological assessment of the trade-off scenario. In this way, the risk to human populations and to the environment are minimized. By contrast, Third World countries lack the technology, infrastructure and capital to deal with hazardous wastes. In addition, since many host countries in the developed world are also producers of toxic wastes they also possess a manpower pool with the necessary experience and background to handle the problems. Third World countries, on the other hand, lack this vital experiential advantage. Despite these drawbacks, many Third World countries are being attracted to the international toxic-waste business by the potential to obtain sub-

stantial infusion of capital into their economies.

The present study focuses upon the problem of toxic-waste transfers and storage as it relates specifically to sub-Saharan Africa. The analysis is approached from two vantage points: first, as an assessment of the potential environmental impacts of toxic waste in the region; second, as an evaluation of the economic rationality of the process based on its benefits and costs, and also in terms of its capacity to generate regional economic development.

As a preface to understanding the motivations that impel sub-Saharan governments to host toxic-waste dumps, the process must be placed within the wider context of several economic realities. The structure of the global market system and the international division of labor do not allow effective participation by African countries in industrial production and exchange; they face worsening terms of trade for their exports, many of which are primary products; national incomes are being systematically strangled by mounting debt obligations; many domestic policies do not demonstrate fiscal responsibility, and internal economic problems are aggravated by World Bank and International Monetary Fund (IMF) economic reform programs (Mengisteab and Logan, 1990; Cornia *et al.*, 1987). The existing environmental, political and socio-economic conditions facing African economies impose serious limitations on prospects for economic development in the region going into the 21st century.

Although the decision to host toxic wastes is related to the underlying problems enumerated above, the process is not necessarily rational, nor is it clear also, that toxic-waste storage is merely another option through which African countries can modify their present economic status. Before meaningful conclusions can be made about these issues, a serious and comprehensive evaluation of the several cost-benefit scenarios of the process must be conducted.

4.

One of the most pervasive features of scientific practice is that scientists gather evidence, by making observations and conducting experiments. This fact provides reason to believe that evidence gathering is a rational means for pursuing scientific goals. Consequently, a philosophy of science which can explain why evidence gathering is a rational means of pursuing scientific goals is (ceteris paribus) to be preferred to one that has no explanation. In this paper I will test several different philosophies of science by examining whether they are able to give such an explanation of why scientists gather evidence.

5.

In designing breeding improvement schemes for farm livestock, there is a well-established series of logical steps to follow (Harris, Stewart and Arboleda, 1984). The first step is to identify the planned production marketing system (or systems) and to define economic merit, which is the breeding objective. The second step is to evaluate available breeding stocks and crosses for economic merit, to choose the best stocks and to derive breeding systems, such as cross-breeding, to exploit them. The next step is to develop testing and selection systems for the further improvement of economic merit. The last step is to disseminate the improved stock to industry so as to enjoy the benefits of the improved work.

This article considers options in designing genetic improvement systems for developing countries. These will, of course, differ for the different species, for different countries and for different production conditions and market needs, ranging from intensive production-marketing systems to subsistence livestock production. The author has no practical experience of breeding work in developing countries, so a rational discussion is attempted though based only on experience with breeding systems in developed countries and on the literature.

6.

We have seen that neither Popper nor Kuhn has any workable explanation of why scientists gather evidence. By contrast, Bayesians have almost an embarrassment of riches, with a number of competing explanations of evidence gathering. As I argued at the beginning of this paper, a satisfactory philosophy of science ought to be able to explain such a central feature as evidence gathering. So from this I draw the conclusion that the ability to explain evidence gathering is a good reason for preferring a Bayesian philosophy of science to a Popperian or Kuhnian philosophy of science.

There are, of course, other non-Bayesian philosophies of science besides those of Popper and Kuhn. In this paper I have thought it best to concentrate on the two most influential non-Bayesian philosophies of science of this century. But though I cannot justify the claim here, I believe that other non-Bayesian philosophies of science (e.g. Feyerabend, Lakatos, and Laudan) are like those of Popper and Kuhn in their inability to explain evidence gathering in science. Consequently, I take the explanation of evidence gathering to be one reason for preferring a Bayesian philosophy of science to any other.

As for those competing Bayesian explanations of evidence gathering, I have argued that the most satisfactory is the one which can be given when we allow that scientists accept hypotheses. I take this to be a reason to make room in Bayesian theory for a notion of acceptance which is not reducible to probability.

7.

In recent years, there has been a growing realization that much more work was required to gear adjustment policies more effectively towards growth. This has been occasioned by the fact that in setting targets for aggregate government spending and ignoring its composition, the quality of expenditure may deteriorate with respect to the growth objective. Indeed, in developing countries, much is made of the potential conflict between adjustment and growth. Too often this has resulted in a call for higher levels of investment, or alternatively, ways have been found to cut recurrent spending to protect the level of capital spending. At the same time, it has often been easier to mobilize the support of the donor community for capital projects than for current spending.

It is now felt that the results of this bias toward capital formation, as opposed to capital maintenance, has generally been damaging to growth. For instance, in developing countries, it is not difficult to find examples of new hospitals being constructed when the old ones cannot operate due to lack of medicines and other supplies, or new roads being constructed while old roads disintegrate through lack of maintenance.

Certainly, from the policy perspective, the emphasis on capital spending is only partly vindicated by the results reported above. Indeed, capital expenditure seems to have exerted its influence through human capital formation rather than through the traditional direct investment channel. For example, the importance of the public provision of infrastructure for growth is not conclusively demonstrated, and the poor relationship between growth and directly productive capital expenditures probably points to the need for better screening of projects to ensure their productivity. Similarly, the importance of going behind aggregate levels to examine the composition of expenditures was also evident in the case of current spending; significantly, current expenditures to maintain the operations of directly productive sectors seemed to have a positive impact on growth. Though it is not possible to draw any firm conclusions from this study, these statistical results do not rule out the possibility that there are certain types of current spending that are even more desirable than capital spending in promoting growth.

8.

This article has tried to demonstrate that, both from an environmental and a socio-economic perspective, the transfer of toxic wastes to sub-Saharan countries has negative implications for the development process. First of all, it is difficult to justify the rationality of the exchange on economic and social grounds because of high levels of uncertainty regarding long-term costs. It is very possible that the benefits for sub-Saharan countries (represented largely by the lease-fee) may be outweighed by the actual and potential environmental and human costs. It is true that the activity offers African countries the opportunity to obtain foreign exchange. However, an economic exchange of this nature is logical for Africa only if it maximises certain opportunities, among them, income-gathering capacity, socio-political stability, social welfare development and environmental stability. The discussion in this article suggests that there are serious uncertainties concerning the ability of toxic-waste dumping to accomplish these goals. Because of the uncertainties concerning long-term costs, it is also difficult to estimate to what extent, and in what way domestic economic opportunities might be created, if at all, by the process. It seems clear that African countries need to establish a policy-structure to minimize the risks associated with the decision-making process. This framework might include at least the following two instruments:

1. A comprehensive environmental impact-assessment which should accompany each application for a land lease.

2. A regional approach based on hydrogeological zones. This would enable neighbouring countries to understand the full scope of potential risks involved when one member decides to host toxic wastes.

> Until a realistic risk-assessment and environmental/human-assessment framework is in place, it is short-sighted policy for African countries to consider toxic-waste dumping to be an economic development strategy.

EXTRACTS TAKEN FROM:
Jack Diamond, 'Government expenditure and growth', *Finance and Development*, December 1990.
Bernard I. Logan, 'An assessment of the environmental and economic implications of toxic-waste disposal in sub-Saharan Africa', *Journal of World Trade*, vol. 25, no. 1, February 1991.
Patrick Maher, 'Why scientists gather evidence', *Brit. J. Phil. Science*, vol. 41, 1990.
C. Smith, 'Genetic improvement of livestock, using nucleus breeding units', *World Animal Review*, January–March 1988.

TASK 10

The text below is the main body of an essay. Read the text and then examine the selection of introductions and conclusions that follow it. Your task will be to decide which of them best suit the text.

The principal reasons for migration have always been economic, though the extent to which an individual is able to make a rational choice to maximise well-being is open to question (Petras, 1981). There have, furthermore, been periods in history when the primary motivation of most migrants in the world was escape from conflict or persecution; in other words, they were refugees. This was the case in the 1940s when millions were displaced in Europe as a result of the Second World War and in India and Pakistan following the partition of India. Though, as the discussion below reveals, non-economic considerations are responsible for a significant number of movements in the world today, income disparities can explain most migration. Over half of the major receiving countries are in economically highly developed regions with per capita GNP of at least $6,900 in 1987, with the exception of Côte d'Ivoire (Arnold, 1990).

The rapid growth of populations in economically less developed countries has put a tremendous strain on infrastructure and employment in their urban areas. The total urban population in these countries is expected to have increased from some 300 million in 1950 to 4 billion in 2025. In many of them, unemployment runs at a level of 30–40 per cent. To prevent this level from rising, 600–700 million jobs will have to be created by the end of the century (Marshall, 1984).

It is worth noting that the rapid population increase in Europe at the end of the nineteenth century was absorbed by permanent emigration to Australia and North America. Today, such emigration constitutes only 2–3 per cent of the population increase in Latin America and very much less in Africa and Asia.

The pressures associated with population growth, particularly in urban areas, are likely to increase the tendency to view emigration as an option while the possibilities for realizing that option become ever more remote. In Mexico, for example, permanent or temporary migration is taken for granted as a means of securing foreign exchange. In fact, it allows such countries to pursue capital and energy intensive policies that would be difficult otherwise (Marshall, 1984). There is little doubt, however, that the industrialised market economies will seek to make immigration more difficult. The organised hiring of foreign unskilled labour in these economies is declining, principally as a result of automation (Bohning, 1984). In other words a potential new workforce of several hundred million in the developing world simply could not be absorbed by the developed world.

Projections of future trends in migration from developing to developed countries indicate that numbers are likely to decline slightly (Arnold, 1990). To the extent that any such estimate is reliable, the decline can be viewed as a reflection of the developed world closing its doors to immigrants rather than any fall in the desire to move.

If we leave aside the economic motive, an examination of other reasons why people migrate in the world today will reveal that their significance is on the increase and of tragic proportions. In 1969, Beijer noted that 'famine, scarcity-of-food induced migration that crosses national frontiers has not been common', with the conspicuous exception of more than a million people going from Ireland to the United States after the famine of the 1840s. In recent decades the number of people displaced by famine has grown dramatically in sub-Saharan Africa, leading to massive movements within countries and between neighbouring countries.

As Jacobson (1989) has noted, a new class of displaced people emerged in the 1980s, namely environmental refugees. An increasing number of people are being affected by ecological catastrophes such as soil degradation, deforestation, drought and flooding. Long droughts in sub-Saharan Africa have already led millions of people to abandon their traditional areas (1.7 billion people in 80 countries are already suffering from serious water shortage). In other areas, an excess of water is forcing people to move in vast numbers. Large parts of the population in coastal areas of countries such as Bangladesh and Egypt face the threat of either having to move or being washed away by floods in the next 30–40 years (Sadik, 1990). Until now, many of these movements have been internal (i.e. within states). The severity of the environmental problems is, however, such that in future those affected are likely to increasingly seek refuge in neighbouring countries. Frequently, countries that generate refugees provide shelter for refugees from other countries.

Migration resulting from war or oppression of a political or religious kind has existed for thousands of years. Although people displaced by natural disasters are today also regarded as refugees, the traditional meaning persists, as reflected in the example of the definition of the Organisation of African Unity:

> … every person, who owing to well founded fear of being persecuted for reasons of race, religion, nationality, membership of a particular social group or political opinion, is outside the country of his nationality and being outside the country of his former habitual residence as the result of such events is unable or, owing to such fear, is unwilling to return to it.
>
> (Melander and Nobel, 1978)

Today, the vast majority of such migrants move from one developing country to another and are mostly victims of internal conflicts. Only in a few instances are they victims of wars between sovereign states. It is very difficult to predict where exactly new conflicts may lead to large outflows of people in politically unstable areas. Neither is it possible to tell easily where there may be a resolution of conflicts leading to repatriation of people who left years earlier, as occurred, for example, in Namibia in 1989. On balance, however, it seems very probable that the number of such migrants will continue to far exceed the comparatively few who are able to return to their own country.

1. Read the following introductions and decide which is the most suitable for the above text.

Introduction 1

> Most movement of people across international boundaries is motivated by economic factors. Petras's model of labour migration seeks to show that patterns of movement are a reflection of the world's division of labour and distribution of wealth. There is a central core of wealthy countries which draws on a pool of reserve labour in a periphery of poor ones. While the motivation of migrants may be economic, there are external factors which constrain the apparent freedom of choice of a person who wants to move.

Introduction 2

> Apart from migrations that occur as a result of war, famine and other disasters, the most common reason for people to move from one country to another is to seek work and improve material well-being.
>
> In this essay, the principal movements occurring across national boundaries in the world today will be examined in the light of economic considerations.

Introduction 3

> The main reasons for international migration are economic. People move because they seek better opportunities of work in wealthier countries. In today's world, this pressure to move is exacerbated by the rapid growth of populations in economically less developed countries. The available manpower cannot be absorbed by the home market and is, thus, increasingly inclined to seek work elsewhere, often following a long-established link of temporary work in a specific developed country.
>
> Besides migration which can be explained by income disparities, there are movements of people resulting from famine and natural disasters. Such movements have tended to increase in recent years, particularly in sub-Saharan Africa where millions have been affected by environmental catastrophes.
>
> Migration caused by conflict or oppression continues to be significant and is mostly the result of internal conflicts.
>
> This essay seeks to examine why most migration trends are not expected to slow down or, at least, not diminish as rapidly as has been predicted.

Introduction 4

Historically, the period of highest international migration occurred in the second half of the nineteenth century and the early part of the twentieth, with the massive outflow of people to North America, mostly from Europe. Between 1845 and 1924, some 50 million people moved. Contrary to popular belief, present movements are not nearly as large. On the other hand, the expectations of experts that international migration would decline rapidly have been proved wrong.

This essay sets out to examine the main reasons why the movements of people across international boundaries have not declined in recent years and are expected to decline at a slower rate than estimated in the near future. Economic considerations still predominate but the continuing significance of migration to escape political conflict or oppression, as well as the enormous growth of movements motivated by environmental disasters, cannot be overlooked.

Migratory pressures have given rise to considerable concern because of the effects on international monetary remittances, the transfer of knowledge and skills and social and political repercussions. Recent studies seem to suggest that migration is being perceived increasingly as a threat to security and stability in many countries. However, a detailed examination of these preoccupations lies outside the scope of this essay.

Introduction 5

Between 1845 and 1924, some 50 million people moved from Europe to North America, representing the period of highest international migration in history. While movements today are not nearly as large, they are still high enough to give cause for concern in a world with diminishing job opportunities both in the developed world, characterised by low population growth but increasing automation, and in the developing world where the population is growing too fast to be absorbed by the home market.

The next part of this essay focuses on the most important reason for migration which is the desire for an improved standard of living.

Introduction 6

'History is written by the winners' a famous writer once stated. Thus we have the phenomenon of people moving from economically depressed to prosperous areas and an emergent literature in the latter chronicling these trends and explaining their growth over the course of this century.

2. Considering both the main body and the introduction you have chosen in question 1, decide which of the following conclusions would be most suitable to end the essay.

Conclusion 1

It is evident that the principal reasons for migration continue to be economic. Migration is one feature of the control wealthy countries exert over the periphery. As automation increases, the hiring of foreign unskilled labour will decline, increasing the burden that developing countries have to absorb a rapidly expanding available workforce into their populations.

It can be concluded that only increased international cooperation will alleviate the problems that emerge as the pressures to migrate in some countries increase and others show reluctance to open their doors to more outsiders.

Conclusion 2

In conclusion, it may be stated that present migration movements, while not nearly as large as those in the past, are still a cause of considerable concern. According to one UN survey on population policy, in 1976 only 6.4 per cent of all the countries in the world regarded their immigration levels as too high; by 1989 the figure was 20.6 per cent.

The expectations of experts that international migration would decline rapidly have been proved wrong. Economic considerations continue to predominate as the reason for moving but political migration and movements resulting from ecological disasters are also important.

Conclusion 3

As I sit in the study, contemplating the silver moon outside my window, I realise that the time has come to end this essay. Movement is the essence of the Universe, whether it be in the dance of the sub-atomic world, the ebbs and flows of the tides, the breezes and gales that move the trees or the migrations of birds and people across land, water and sky. It is nomads who have always remained closest to the essential nature of man in responding to the inner call to be always on the move. The movements of people across boundaries are simply an atavistic reflection of this response.

Conclusion 4

There is little doubt that international migration will be a serious problem for years to come. Like other problems that affect a wide range of countries, the solution to this one cannot be found easily. However, through increasing cooperation, on a worldwide scale, perhaps the situation will improve in a relatively short space of time. Needless to say, it will not be easy but then there are no ready-made solutions to problems of this magnitude. It will require considerable human ingenuity and good will. I hope the efforts will not be in vain.

Conclusion 5

This essay has touched on the reasons why migration movements cannot be expected to diminish dramatically in the near future.

It can be seen that economic considerations prevail in determining movements of people across international boundaries. As the available labour force in developing countries increases and the markets in those countries are increasingly unable to absorb new people, there is likely to be increasing pressure to seek opportunities abroad. However, in the industrialised economies the need for unskilled foreign labour, which has been considerable in the past, is declining due to automation.

Movements resulting from famine have increased, particularly in sub-Saharan Africa. In addition, a new kind of migration has emerged as a result of environmental disasters; however, this kind of movement has mostly been confined within countries.

People are still forced to move as a result of conflicts and oppression, a type of migration that is unlikely to subside in the foreseeable future, given the instability that persists in many areas of the world.

Conclusion 6

One can conclude that, despite the uncertainties of making predictions, the pressures to move for economic reasons are likely to increase but the number of people able to move may be constrained by the reluctance of many industrialised countries to accept as many migrants as they have in the past.

In the developing world, migration resulting from natural disasters or political upheaval is unlikely to diminish.

As far as policy implications are concerned, a greater contribution to decreasing migration movements may lie in maintaining peace and economic stability, globally and regionally, rather than measures designed to limit movements to individual countries.

Task 11

Look at the five descriptions of different kinds of synthesis of references from more than one source (a–e). Then read the short extracts of academic writing that follow. Choose the description that best suits each extract.

(a) A simple presentation of supporting information from two sources.

(b) A presentation of several differing viewpoints with some added comment by the writer.

(c) An incorporation of several viewpoints which are then challenged by the writer.

(d) Opposing viewpoints from two principal sources which are incorporated to support a point made by the writer.

(e) Several viewpoints which are used to discredit or weaken a point made by the writer.

Extract 1

T. H. Huxley (7) claimed that 'science is nothing but trained and organised common sense', a view supported by Whitehead (17). It has, however, been strongly argued that scientific method cannot possibly be based on common sense. Wolpert (19) points out that simple observation of everyday life phenomena will not lead us to scientifically valid explanations. In fact, he goes as far as to maintain that ideas which fit common sense will not be scientifically correct. One might conclude that one reason why scientific discovery was so slow for so many centuries was precisely because it tended to avoid imaginative speculation far removed from commonplace thinking.

Extract 2

According to Popper (1968: 172), scientific discovery occurs in an 'open society' with a standard of objectivity that is rigorous and unfailingly reliable. Kuhn (1962: 166), on the other hand, suggests that the scientific community is a totalitarian one. It is apparent from his view that a theory which does not conform to a prevailing orthodoxy will be rejected, even if it seems acceptable along the lines of the sort of criteria Popper would adhere to for scientific validity.

Fleck (1935), whose ideas strongly influenced Kuhn, acknowledged that a scientist such as Einstein may have gone about his scientific investigation in quite a unique way. However, his view was that the significance of Einstein's contribution to physics could be understood only in the light of the shared objectives and standards of the academic community in physics (Toulmin, 1986: 276).

Extract 3

The 'sovereignty at bay' thesis of multinationals maintained that while the expansion of these companies constrained the power of nation-states, the overall effects of such expansion was internationally beneficial (Vernon, 1968, 1971). Two observers, Ball (1967) and Johnson (1970), even went as far as to suggest that the recognition of the benefits of multinationals might spearhead moves for world economic integration that would lead to further erosion of the nation-state.

Subsequent experience has shown that nation-states are capable of considerable resilience against multinationals. Moreover, the idea of international economic integration in a world in which the 500 largest multinational corporations control 70 per cent of total world trade may have somewhat different implications from what was envisaged by observers in a more optimistic era.

Extract 4

As far back as 1860, Herbert Spencer observed that laughter released tension and had good effects on human health. This view was supported by Cousins (3), who wrote a best-selling book describing how he cured himself from a chronic disease of the spine. He attributed his recovery to watching films that made him laugh and large intakes of vitamin C. This led him to speculate that the beneficial properties of laughter were related to pituitary secretions known as endorphins which reduce pain as well as inducing euphoria.

Extract 5

It is very tempting to assume that the pagan mysteries were easy to understand on account of their widespread popularity. It may be that on the level of a popular initiation ritual, such festivals as the one at Eleusis had symbols that appeared to be clear and certain. However, Wind is quick to make the distinction between such meanings and what he describes as 'figurative' and 'magic' ones (16). The revival of interest in the mysteries that is very evident in the writings of Italian Renaissance thinkers certainly seemed to favour a 'figurative' understanding, even if a range of views existed. One need not go as far as Pico della Mirandola, who appeared to insist that mysteries must be obscure to be profound. Calcagnini dismissed the case for deliberate obscurity while acknowledging the wisdom of riddles (Wind, 20).

Task 12

Read the two texts below and then extract in note form all the information that is necessary to write a short essay of comparison and contrast on the following topic:

> **Kahn and Heilbronner: Two different versions of the future**

(At the end of the essay you can add some comments of your own on the basis of your own observations.)

Text 1

Popular forecasts of future global development in the period after World War II tended to be optimistic until the early 1970s (Clarke, 1964; Kahn, 1967; Clark, 1970). It can be no accident that the emergence of highly gloomy predictions coincided with a downturn in economic performance, characterised by recession and high inflation. These predictions represented, in different degrees, a reversal to Malthusian thinking, with the prevailing view that supplies of food and resources would be outstripped by population growth.

Though Herman Kahn's first study of the future appeared in the sixties (Kahn and Wiener, 1967), he continued to contribute to an optimistic vision, albeit a more qualified one, until his death in 1983 (Kahn and Bruce-Briggs, 1972; Kahn, Brown and Martel, 1976; Simon and Kahn, 1984). In the meantime, a large number of studies predicted troubled times ahead, if not wholesale catastrophe. In the United States, the much-publicised work of Ehrlich (1970), Forrester (1971), Meadows (1974) and Heilbronner (1974) culminated at the end of the seventies with the 'Global 2000 Report to the President' (1980), to which Kahn's last work was a response.

Kahn's work at the Hudson Institute came under sharp attack for being unrealistic (Dumont, 1974), and for trying to promote a very Westernised model of development. The latter criticism is undoubtedly valid. It is less clear to what extent any propagandism was conscious, despite accusations that the research was funded by very conservative interests. However, it is not true that Kahn and his associates overlooked major human problems. They simply had enormous faith in humankind's resourcefulness and capacity to find a solution to these problems.

Even if growth continued at rates predicted by more pessimistic forecasts, the world was seen as being able to support a much larger population. Shortages of food were seen as being an outcome of mismanagement rather than of any limits to food technology. If the environment underwent degradation, new techniques would be found to preserve it. In about 100–200 years, there would be a levelling-off in world population and economic growth. In the meantime, continuing growth and wealth in the developed countries would gradually bring about better living standards for an increasing number of people around the whole world, even if the wealth continued to be unequally distributed. In short, Kahn's tendency was to always look on the bright side.

Contrary to expectations, Kahn's studies did predict problems such as the possibility of widespread starvation. They also saw conflicts, at least on a small scale, as inevitable. Moreover, there was considerable uncertainty with respect to the future of poorer nations (Kahn and Weiner, 1967). It is also worth noting that any positive outcomes were not expected to be achieved without effort. The conclusions were 'reassuring, though not grounds for complacency' (Simon and Kahn, 1984).

Text 2

Robert Heilbronner's vision of the future changed from a confidently optimistic one in the early 1960s to bleak pessimism a decade later. In 'An Enquiry into the Human Prospect' (1974), he saw the inevitability of an eventual decline in industrial growth in the developed world because of limits to resources. Such a decline was likely to increase tensions between rich and poor nations greatly. In the latter, continuing population growth would increase pressures, lowering living standards drastically as food and other resources became more scarce. The solution in the short run was to encourage technical advancement for as long as possible. Time was limited but it was a mistake to curtail growth immediately, denying the possibility for minimal improvement in the most underdeveloped areas as well as new discoveries which might stave off shortages of resources.

Heilbronner saw environmental disaster in the form of global warming as a strong possibility. This necessitated the adoption of pollution-free technology, which would mean further limiting of industrial production. He predicted that the way to prevent misuse of resources and the environment would be through authoritarian government, which might be unpopular but was the alternative to anarchy.

This view was among the most pessimistic of a number of 'scenarios' which emerged in the space of a few years (see, for example, Meadows, 1974). Underlying it, there is a fairly bleak theory of human nature. Heilbronner observes that human beings tend to acquiesce in political authority because it gives them a sense of security. He also sees a tendency for most people in every society to limit their concern for others to a group. The size of this group becomes larger in adulthood but a capacity to exclude concern from non-members seems to be inherent in human nature.

TASK 13

Drawing on information from the two articles below, write a short essay on the following topic:

What did Professor Durant's surveys reveal about public knowledge of science and scientific method in Britain?

The gulf between Professor Boffin and Joe Public

Susan Young meets a scientist dedicated to overcoming people's awe – and fear – of science.

THE trouble with scientific education in this country, says Professor John Durant, is that it is geared to producing future researchers and academic high-flyers. What it does not do is produce school-leavers who are scientifically literate, possessing the basic tools of understanding.

'Most people in this country can read and write, and the reason is because universal education instils the principles into most children. If we are going to have a scientifically literate population – people who can find their way around the world of science in a reasonably competent way – then first and foremost it's the responsibility of schools to instil the basics,' he says. 'The notion of literacy is very relevant. Reading and writing is an enormous asset, but we don't describe someone as literate if they are just deeply familiar with a particular book like *Tom Sawyer*.'

It is something which concerns Durant: indeed, it is his life's work. As Assistant Director of the Science Museum and Imperial College's Professor in the Public Understanding of Science, his job for the past three years has been to work out exactly why there is such an enormous gulf between what tabloids still refer to as 'boffins' and their readers.

The paradox is that in an increasingly technological age we need to be more aware of science – but instead, many people are baffled by it. Few owners of such commonplace kitchen gadgets as microwaves can explain how they work, and ignorance breeds fear – such as that described by one woman interviewed by Durant who wondered if she shouldn't cook the family meals wearing a lead apron.

One of Durant's surveys, which compared basic scientific knowledge on both sides of the Atlantic, found just 31 per cent of Britons and 43 per cent of Americans knew electrons are smaller than atoms. Almost a third of Britons and almost a quarter of Americans believe antibiotics kill viruses as well as bacteria – despite a far higher interest in matters medical rather than other branches of science among both groups.

Although statistically the average scores of both groups turned out to be similar – 9.26 correct answers out of 15 for the British and 10.02 for the Americans – detailed results were more worrying. The survey, published in 1989, discovered that 34 Britons gave two or fewer correct answers, against only three Americans – and this on a quiz that included what the authors described as 'morale-boosting' questions such as 'the centre of the earth is very hot'. At the other end of the scale, 91 Americans but only 11 Britons got top marks.

But Durant does not think rote-learning of yet more scientific 'facts' in schools is the answer.

'The world is a fast-changing place and even people who have stayed at school until 18 will find their knowledge is out of date by the time they are 28. Ten years is a long time in science. The media, museums and so on all play a part in keeping people up to date, but they need the basic grounding.

'School should be a foundation. I think the problem we have still got with the education system in general in this country is that it is geared to the principle of training an élite who are going to become highly skilled or perhaps even professional scientists.

'Compare it with the teaching of music, for instance, and you would be giving all schoolchildren the training of concert violinists. An education designed for maximum benefit would be for the understanding of music – musical appreciation, if you like.'

What Durant would like to see children given is a greater understanding of what science is really like, how it works and how it affects everyday life – 'whether eggs contain salmonella or are safe to eat, what happened at Chernobyl and so on'.

(*The Observer*, 2.2.92.)

Surveying the extent of public ignorance

THE British survey, carried out by John Durant and his colleagues at the University of Oxford in 1988, makes gloomy reading, at least at first glance. Not only were many of the people sampled unable to answer some of the questions probing their knowledge of scientific facts, but very few, Durant says, seemed to understand what it means 'to study something scientifically': only 3 per cent of the 2000 people questioned associated science with testing theories, for example.

But less abstract questions revealed that many people did indeed have an idea of what 'scientific method' is meant to be. For example, when respondents were asked to decide between alternative ways in which a doctor might be sure a drug was working, almost two-thirds opted for a comparison between people taking a drug and those not taking a drug – the basis of clinical trials.

Durant also discovered that people were twice as likely to pick the right answer (quoting an experimental comparison) if the question was medical. People faced with a similar question about comparing two metals were more likely to pick the 'wrong' answer, and conclude that the practitioner would rely on a prior knowledge of metals. As Durant says, 'people don't know what metallurgists do'.

People are not only more familiar with medicine, but, to the researchers' surprise, they also see it as 'very scientific'. When people were asked to rank different disciplines as more or less rigorously scientific, medicine was given a higher 'scientific' rating even than physics.

When Durant and his colleagues looked more closely at these data they found that those who did better on their factual knowledge ('science understanding' scores) were more likely to discriminate between the disciplines of science. High rating for medicine came predominantly from those whose 'understanding' scores were low.

Beliefs about science in turn owe much to media accounts, and newspapers and TV probably devote more coverage to advances in medicine than to other fields. Jean-Marie Trouve, at the University of Poitiers, argues that, in France at least, the media tend to portray physics and chemistry exclusively through their industrial and technological applications. This might explain the results of his survey, which suggested that many French people see physics and chemistry as technology. The French media portray medicine, on the other hand, as scientific; we can speculate, Trouve suggests, that 'studies of the human body and mind will occupy the vacuum left by hard sciences and become Science par excellence'.

It is easy, too, to misinterpret surveys by assuming that people always act on their professed beliefs. Jon Miller at the Public Opinion Laboratory at the University of Northern Illinois conducted similar surveys for the American National Science Foundation. Disturbing though it seems that more than a third of adult Americans sampled thought astrology to be scientific, few (about 5 per cent) actually *used* astrological prediction to guide what they did. Yet three-quarters said that they used scientific information from animal testing of drugs and food to change what food or medicines they consumed.

(Lynda Birke, 'The perils of popular science', *The New Scientist*, 18.8.90.)

UNIT 4

TOWARDS EXTENDED WRITING

MAIN SKILLS	TASKS CORRESPONDING TO SKILLS
THE INCLUSION OF TABLES AND FIGURES	TASK 1
WRITING A BIBLIOGRAPHY	TASKS 2 + 3
EXTENDED WRITING	TASK 4

AIMS

The main aim of this unit is to produce a piece of writing based on library research in your own subject area. You will need to incorporate and extend the skills practised in Units 1–3 and this unit. You should ensure that you have an adequate command of these skills. At the end of Unit 5, you will be expected to write a more detailed essay. The one in this unit should be an introduction to your subject, or an area of your subject, for the non-specialist.

Before embarking on the extended writing you will need to consider:

1. the inclusion of tables and figures in an academic paper
2. the layout of written work (title and contents page, bibliography etc.)
3. the stages of extended writing.

1. TABLES AND FIGURES IN AN ACADEMIC PAPER

In your essay you may wish to present data of a statistical nature, (as well as diagrams, drawings or maps). Statistical data are most clearly presented in the form of tables or graphs. Any graphic illustration which is not a table is known as a *figure*. This includes graphs, maps, diagrams, drawings and photographs.

The inclusion of tables and/or figures in an essay or paper should help to clarify or expand an appropriate section of the text. However, you should also ensure that information contained in tables or figures is self-sufficient and can be understood independently of the text.

Tables and figures should be placed as near to the relevant part of the text as possible, but they should not precede the discussion of them in the text. If the table or figure is relatively small, then it may appear within the body of the text. However, large tables and figures are usually placed on a separate page from the body. A title, or caption, is given to each. In the case of a table, this appears above the table, (e.g. *Table 1*), and in the case of an illustration, it appears below the illustration (e.g. *Figure 1*). If there is a series of tables or illustrations in your work, these should form a separate section and appear in the table of contents at the beginning of your paper.

In addition to selecting a suitable position for tables and figures, you must also *refer* to them in the main body of the text. This may be done quite simply; for example, after the relevant discussion, you can write in brackets: '(see Figure 1)'. You can also make the reference part of a sentence: 'Figure 1 shows …'. As with quotations, be selective when introducing tables or figures. They should be appropriate to the discussion and enhance the reader's understanding of the text.

2. LAYOUT OF WRITTEN WORK

It is important that you present your work properly. Your department will expect this during your course of study. Although conventions vary from department to department, the expected layout will probably approximate to the one below:

Title page	
Abstract	
Table of contents	prelims
List of tables and figures (if any)	
Introduction	
Main body	main text
Conclusion (or discussion)	
Appendices (if any)	end matter
Bibliography	

The above will all be identified by headings, except the main body. The material should be type-written or written legibly by hand, and presented with the following:

- A4 paper
- Margins
- Double spacing
  Written on one side of the paper only
- Numbered pages
- Indentation or triple spacing for new paragraphs.

Examples of well laid out title and contents pages follow.

MICROBIAL ACTIVITY IN FOOD

by Angela M. D. Fernandes

1988

TABLE OF CONTENTS

DELTAIC DEPOSITIONAL SYSTEMS

An Introduction

BY
A. TURHAN

8 SEPTEMBER, 1988

Centre for Applied Language Studies
Language Resource Centre
University of Reading, Whiteknights, Reading, England

CONTENTS

The main appendix is a section containing additional factual or explanatory information. It usually appears immediately after the main body of the text. Mention of an appendix should appear in the table of contents.

COMPILING A BIBLIOGRAPHY

It is useful to get into the habit of compiling a bibliography with full details as soon as you start to find books or articles on a topic. It may seem unnecessary (particularly for a short paper) to have such complete references; however, you may find that later, when you want to refer to a particular book or article, lack of information makes it impossible or time-consuming. If you keep an accurate record of your references (for example, on your note cards), it will be an easy task to include references in the body of your work and to write up the bibliography.

Bibliographical entries normally follow a strict format, although this format may vary from one subject area to another. You will have to check what the preferences are in your subject or department – for example, with respect to the order of entries (normally alphabetical according to author's surname) or the writing of the surname (often in capital letters).

Below are some generally accepted suggestions. Look carefully at the punctuation given in the examples, and use the examples as a guideline for your bibliographies. It is important that you always give all the information which someone else would need to find the item.

A book

You must record the following:

- author
- date of publication
- title
- publisher
- place of publication (useful where the publisher is not well-known, or where there are British and American editions etc.).

The first and most important item in a bibliography is the surname of the author. Surnames are listed in alphabetical order. If there are several authors/editors, the book is listed under the surname of the first author/editor. If the book is edited, make sure you indicate this by putting (ed.) or (eds) after the name(s).

Examples

(a) Author (surname first) Date *Title* (underlined or in italics). Place: Publisher.
   Allen, J. R. L. 1985 *Principles of Physical Sedimentology*. London: Allen & Unwin.

(b) Author, *Title*, Publisher, Place. Date.
   Bourne, M. C. *Food Texture and Viscosity: Concept and Measurement*, Academic Press, New York. 1982.

(c) Author (Date), *Title*, Place: Publisher.
   White, Ron (1986) *Writing Away*, London: Lingual House.

If the entry for a book/article runs over more than one line, subsequent lines should be indented to make the surname stand out, as in (a) and (b) above.

If there is more than one publication by the same author, the earlier one comes first. If the author wrote two books in one year, these are listed 1978a, 1978b (for example) *a* being the one which is mentioned first in *your* work.

Example
Grindy, A. P. 1975(a) *Mathematical Statistics.* Oxford: OUP.
_____ 1975(b) *Medical Statistics.* Oxford: OUP.

Where you refer to an article in a collected edition, the editors of the book are mentioned and the title of the *book* is underlined or italicised (not the article).

Example
Author (Date) Title of article (Editors) *Name of book,* Place: Publisher.
Grice, H. P. (1975) Logic and conversation, in Cole, P. & Morgan, J. (eds) *Syntax and Semantics 3: Speech Acts,* New York: Academic Press.

A journal article

You must record the following:

- author
- date
- title of the article
- full title of the journal
- volume number
- issue number
- page reference.

Where you refer to an article in a journal, the title of the *journal* is underlined or italicised and the volume and page numbers are given.

Example
Author Date 'Title of article', *Journal* (underlined or in italics), Volume number./ Issue number: Pages.

Williams, R. 1986 ' "Top Ten" principles for teaching reading', *ELT Journal,* 40/1: 42–45.

Unpublished works

Example
Rignall, M. 1991 *Oral Narratives in English and Greek.* Unpublished M.A. thesis (C.A.L.S., University of Reading).

Note: Remember to underline or italicise the title of the book/journal (*not* the title of an article).

Bibliography

You must include a bibliography or list of references at the end of every piece of academic writing. Several variations exist depending on the system you have used to refer to other writers in your work (see Unit 3, especially Task 11). If you list only works that you have referred to in your essay, you should entitle your list 'References' (or 'Works cited', a title favoured in the Humanities). The title 'Bibliography' is used when, in addition to sources cited in your essay, you also include background reading you have not cited.

Finally, look at the example of a short bibliography below. Variations on this format are acceptable – check what the particular demands are for submitting bibliographies in your subject area. Remember that your final objective, when you have completed all the tasks in the next section, will be to produce a bibliography in your own subject area.

ALLEN J. R. L. (1970) *Physical Processes of Sedimentation: An Introduction*, London: George Allen and Unwin Ltd.

ALLEN J. R. L. (1970) Sediments of the modern Niger delta: a summary and review, in Morgan J. P. and Shaver R. H. (eds), *Deltaic Sedimentation: Modern and Ancient*, Tulsa, Oklahoma, USA: Society of Economic Paleontologists and Mineralogists, Special Publication No. 15, pp. 138–51.

DOORNKAMP J. C. and KRINSLEY D. (1971) Electron microscopy applied to quartz grains from a tropical environment, *Sedimentology*, 17, pp. 89–101.

FRIEND P. F. and MOODY-STUART M. (1970) Carbonate deposition on the river flood plains of the Wood Bay Formation (Devonian) of Spitsbergen, *Geol. Mag.*, 107, pp. 181–95.

READING H. G. (1981) *Sedimentary Environments and Facies*, Oxford: Blackwell Scientific Publications.

SELLEY R. C. (1976) *An Introduction to Sedimentology*, London: Academic Press.

WHITTOW J. (1988) *Dictionary of Physical Geography*, London: Penguin Books Ltd.

3. THE STAGES OF EXTENDED WRITING

There are five main stages in writing an extended essay:

  (a) Preliminary outline
  (b) Research
  (c) First draft
  (d) Revising
  (e) Final draft.

(a) PRELIMINARY OUTLINE

A preliminary outline is a plan of work which should help you clarify your thoughts on your chosen topic for extended writing and help you plan the various sections of your paper. It will also help you assess the strengths and weaknesses of your ideas and allow you to revise them later.

First, you have to decide on a topic. Until now you may only have had some vague ideas of what you will write about and have probably acquired a few references as well as writing a summary of a chapter or article (see the end of Unit 2). When you have a clearer idea of a topic, you might like to brainstorm ideas about it with your colleagues or teacher. If you are uncertain about what topic to choose, try to get access to course outlines from your future department. Alternatively, it may be possible to look through some recent research journals or subject specialist journals for ideas.

Now take a piece of paper and note down any thoughts, questions or ideas you have concerning the topic. These need not be in any specific order. Organise your ideas into a preliminary outline of main sections and sub-sections, using any method that suits you: a skeleton or a mind-map, for example.

Study your preliminary outline. Delete any ideas you consider irrelevant or insufficiently related to the main topic. Can you improve on it in any other ways? For example:

- Are any sections too long or insufficient?
- Are main sections of equal weight and importance?
- Do you have sufficient sub-sections to support each main point?
- Do you wish to reorganise the order of the main body or any sub-sections?

(b) RESEARCH

Having made a preliminary outline, you will now need to spend a lot of time in reading, data-collecting and note-taking. Remember to note sources of information and all bibliographical references in full.

As you research your paper, you will probably discover new lines of thought or find that some areas are deficient in data or need more detailed treatment. This will necessitate modifying your preliminary outline. Furthermore, as you progress through your research, you will find that new ideas concerning alternative approaches will suggest themselves to you. Make a note of these for future reference as you may wish to incorporate them into your essay. As you collect your data, use note cards (see Unit 2).

(c) FIRST DRAFT

When you think you have sufficient data you should begin writing your first draft. Your note cards should prove very useful here. You will be able to order your cards to follow your preliminary outline of main topics and sub-topics. Study the cards thoroughly. Have you decided on the best arrangement? Do you have insufficient cards for any particular sections? If so, a little more research will be necessary.

When writing, you do not necessarily have to begin with Section 1. Begin with the section you feel most confident about. Having got some of your ideas down on paper, you will find it easier to progress to the next sections. Write from your note cards in simple English. If you write on alternate lines on one side of the paper only, this will enable you to note corrections, amendments, additions etc. more easily later. However, at this stage concentrate on getting your ideas down on paper rather than spending time thinking whether you can express your ideas in a better way. Do not worry if, at this stage, you cannot find the exact word or phrase that you need.

(d) REVISING

You will need to allow time for re-reading, re-shaping and re-thinking your ideas. If possible, leave your work for a time. This will allow your mind to re-process your ideas, and when you return to your work, you will be able to do so more clearly and more objectively.

Read through your first draft. It may have been perfectly clear to you as the writer at the time of writing, but it may not be clear, logical and well organised to the reader. Leaving your work for a while will enable you to perceive any difficulties for the reader. Check the order and clarity of your ideas, paragraphs and sections. You might find it necessary to re-order and revise your writing to ensure that your ideas are more effectively presented and logically connected. If any parts of your writing are unclear, is it because you have plagiarised source material or attempted to paraphrase it without a complete understanding?

If possible, ask a colleague to read your draft and suggest any improvements. This can be very useful in helping to revise a first draft. This practice is emphasised in the Writing book in this series, which also has checklists to help you with revising.

(e) FINAL DRAFT

(a) Read through your revised draft. Do you need to make any more changes? Have you positioned tables or figures correctly, and have you referred to these within the body of the text? Have quotations and references to other writers been incorporated correctly?

As you read, note down any major points you wish to mention in your introduction and conclusion.

(b) Write the introduction and conclusion. Writing the introduction may help you to give a structure to the main body of your essay if you have had trouble doing so.

(c) Write a final copy. Make sure that you have included any changes or improvements that you feel are necessary.

(d) Read through your final draft. Have you left your reader with the feeling that this is a *complete* piece of work? Check that the contents page matches the text in every detail.

(e) Compile your bibliography. This is easily done by arranging your bibliography cards in alphabetical order. Check that all references within the body of the text are indicated and that you have included all the necessary details in the bibliographical section.

UNIT 4 *TOWARDS EXTENDED WRITING: TASKS*

TASK 1

Look at the list of titles below and choose the most suitable one as a caption for each figure or table on the following pages. Remembering that the discussion should precede the illustration, write a short paragraph which could be placed before each figure or table, referring to the information in it.

- Air pollution: emissions of black smoke, sulphur dioxide and nitrogen oxides
- The gender composition of the UK population
- Destination of first degree students
- Air and rail passenger transport use
- The relative contribution to the greenhouse effect of various gases
- Students in further education by sex and type
- Road and rail passenger transport use
- Registered full-time students at the University of Reading by sex and type, 1992–93.

a.

	Undergraduate		Postgraduate	
	Men	Women	Men	Women
Letters and Social Sciences	1245	2010	211	257
Science	925	438	338	134
Agriculture and Food	291	289	218	112
Urban and Regional Studies	628	245	83	35
Education and Community Studies	140	672	214	331
	3,229	*3,654*	*1,064*	*869*

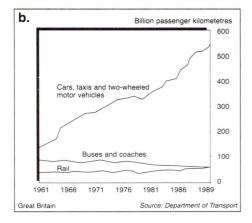

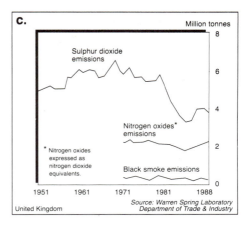

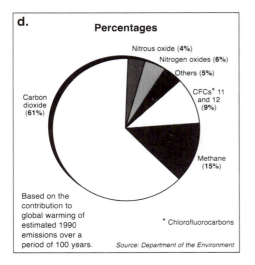

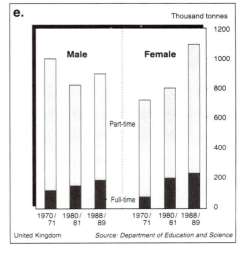

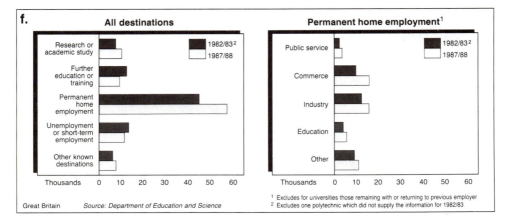

TASK 2

IDENTIFYING BIBLIOGRAPHICAL REFERENCES

Look at the bibliographical entries below.

(a) State whether they are for a book, article etc.
(b) What do the numbers in brackets refer to (e.g. date of publication etc.)?

1. (1)   (1)   (2)

    Kosai, Yutaka and Ogino, Yoshitaro (1984) *The Contemporary Japanese*
    (3)
    Economy. London: Macmillan.

2. (1)

    Weiner, Myron (1971) 'Political integration & political development', in
    (2)   (3)
    Finkle, J. L. & Gable, R. W. (eds) *Political Development and Social Change*. New
    York: John Wiley.

3. (1)

    National Research Council, Committee on Research Priorities in Tropical
    (2)
    Biology (1980) *Research Priorities in Tropical Biology*. Washington DC:
    (3)
    Academic Sciences.

4. (1)

    Elston, C. D. (1981) 'The financing of Japanese industry', *Bank of England*
    (2)   (3)   (4)
    Quarterly Bulletin 21, 4:510–518.

5. (1)   (2)   (3)

    Mason, A. (1990) 'Politics and the state', *Political Studies* XXXVIII, 575–87.

TASK 3

COMPILING A BIBLIOGRAPHY

Look at the following extract from a bibliography and decide in what ways it is inadequate or incomplete. Full details of all the items except the first one are to be found on different pages in this book.

BLOOMFIELD, L. (1964) Literate and illiterate speech. In Hymes, D. (Ed.) *Language in Culture and Society*, New York: Harper and Row.

DULAY, H., BURT, M. and KRASHEN, S. (1982) Language Two, Oxford University Press.

STERN, H. H. (1983) *Fundamental Concepts of Language Teaching*, Oxford.

RAIMES, A. (1985) What unskilled ESL students do as they write: a classroom study of composing, *TESOL Quarterly*.

WHITE, R. V. *The ELT Curriculum: Design, Innovation and Management*, Oxford and New York: Basil Blackwell.

TASK 4

Look at the following bibliographies produced by students at the end of an essay on theories in modern physics. Which of them are acceptable?

Bibliography 1

BOHM, D. *Quantum Theory.* New York, Prentice Hall, 1951.
BOHM, D. *Wholeness and the Implicate Order.* London, Routledge and Kegan Paul, 1988.
BOHR, N. *Atomic Physics and Human Knowledge.* New York, John Wiley and Sons, 1958.
EINSTEIN, A. *Ideas and Opinions,* Seeling, C. (ed.). New York, Dell Publishing Co., 1973.
HAWKING, S. and GIBBONS, G. W. 'Cosmological event horizons, thermodynamics and particle creation', *Physical Review* D, Vol. 15, No. 10, 15th May, 1977, pp. 2738–56.
HAWKING, S. *Is The End In Sight For Theoretical Physics?* Cambridge University Press, 1980.
HOLTON, G. 'Mach, Einstein and the search for reality', *Daedalus,* Vol. 97, Spring, 1968, pp. 636–73.
ROSS, G. Macdonald *Leibniz.* Oxford University Press, 1984.

Bibliography 2

BOHM, D. (1951) *Quantum Theory,* New York: Prentice Hall.
BOHM, D. (1980) *Wholeness and the Implicate Order,* London: Routledge and Kegan Paul.
BOHR, N. (1958) *Atomic Physics and Human Knowledge,* New York: John Wiley and Sons.
EINSTEIN, A. (1973) *Ideas and Opinions,* Seeling, C. (ed.), New York: Dell Publishing Co.
HAWKING, S. (1980) *Is The End In Sight For Theoretical Physics?* Cambridge: Cambridge University Press.
HAWKING, S. (1988) *A Brief History of Time: From the Big Bang to Black Holes,* London: Bantam.
HAWKING, S. and GIBBONS, G. W. (1977) 'Cosmological event horizons, thermodynamics and particle creation', *Physical Review* D. Vol. 15, No. 10, 15th May, pp. 2738–2756.
HOLTON, G. (1968) 'Mach, Einstein and the search for reality', *Daedalus* Vol. 97, Spring, pp. 636–73.
ROSS, G. MACDONALD (1984) *Leibniz,* Oxford: Oxford University Press.

Bibliography 3

'Atomic Physics and Human Knowledge', N. Bohr (1958).

'Is The End In Sight For Theoretical Physics?' S. Hawking (1980) Cambridge University Press, Cambridge.

'Cosmological Event Horizons, Thermodynamics and Particle Creation', S. Hawking and G. W. Gibbons, Physical Review D15 (1977).

'Ideas and Opinions', Albert Einstein, C. Seeling (ed.) (1973).

'Leibniz', George McDonald Ross (1984).

'Mach, Einstein and the search for reality', G. Holton, Daedalus 97 (1968).

'Quantum Theory', D. Bohm (1951).

'Wholeness and the Implicate Order', D. Bohm (1980).

TASK 5

Look at the items below. Check that information in each reference is in the correct order and then list all the references in alphabetical order as a bibliography.

'International migration: who goes where?' Fred Arnold, Finance and Development, vol. 27, no. 2, June 1990, pp.46–7.

N. Sadik, The State of the World Population 1990 (New York: UN Population Fund, 1990).

Ray Marshall: 'Immigration: an international economic perspective', International Migration Review, vol. xviii, no. 3, 1984, pp.593–5

Ed. J. A. Jackson, Migration, Cambridge University Press, 1969.

Environmental Refugees: A yardstick of habitability, (Washington D.C., Worldwatch Institute, 1989), J. L. Jacobson.

'The global labour market in the modern world economy', E. Petras, in Global Trends in Migration, eds. M. M. Kritz, C. B. Keely and S. M. Tomasi (1981), New York, Center for Migration Studies.

Bohning, W. R. (London, Macmillan, 1984), Studies in International Migration.

Melander G. and P. Nobel (eds.), African Refugees and the Law, Uppsala, Scandinavian Institute of African Studies, 1978.

Widgren Jonas, (1990), 'International migration and regional stability', International Affairs, 66, 4, (1990) pp. 749–66.

TASK 6

The aim of this task is to produce a piece of work of between 800 and 1,300 words, based, where possible, on different source materials. The aim is to provide a general introduction to a main topic area in your subject specialisation or a general introduction to the subject you intend to study.

1. Select a main topic area from your intended course of study.
2. Highlight and discuss important problems and issues in topic area.

UNIT 5

WRITING THE EXTENDED ESSAY

MAIN SKILLS	TASKS CORRESPONDING TO SKILLS
EXTENDED WRITING	MAIN TASK
REVISING	ADDITIONAL TASK

AIMS

The main aim of this unit is to produce an extended piece of writing based on research in your subject area. The topic chosen should be more specific than for your essay at the end of Unit 4 and should be treated in greater depth. You should approach the work as if you were asked to produce a piece of work by your future department on your main course.

Prior to the written work you will discuss the 'Guide' section with your teacher. This focuses on:

1. Choosing a topic
2. Collecting data
3. Writing the paper
4. Writer's block
5. Revising
6. Proof-reading
7. Abbreviations commonly used in academic writing.

1. CHOOSING A TOPIC

It may be difficult to select a topic for a piece of extended writing. This may be because the area of study is new to you, or because you roughly know the area you are interested in but are not sure what topic to follow up. Various approaches for selecting a topic are suggested below. You might like to combine a variety of these, assuming you have access to subject specialist sources.

Find out what has been done before. You can do this in several ways:

(a) Refer to your department.
- Consult a course outline.
- Discuss areas of interest with your tutor/fellow students.
- Browse through previous dissertations of predecessors on higher degree courses.

(b) Go to a university or college library.
- Look through some research journals.
- Consult a catalogue and look under specific topic areas.
- Skim through an index to theses accepted for higher degrees by universities in an English-speaking country.

Once you have found out what has been done on the subject it will be easier for you to identify a gap in a well-researched area you are interested in. Now write down a brief title for your essay. It is important for you to do this before you do more reading as you may have now found which direction to follow. If you do not write the title down, you may feel an area has been over-researched and has nothing more to offer, when in fact an interesting gap in the research exists that you may be able to fill.

2. COLLECTING DATA

If your chosen topic is a new field of study or you have discovered a gap in research, you may find there is a *lack* of literature relating specifically to your chosen area. If this is the case, consider what line of research you should follow. What problems do you envisage? How far will current literature and research relate to this new area? Will you need to carry out primary research (e.g. experiments, interviews, questionnaires) to support your ideas?

(a) Discover important sources.

- Consult your department as to any recognised authorities or important published works.
- Consult a library catalogue for authors who have published books and for collected editions of articles in your area.
- Follow up references in your reading. Familiar references which occur repeatedly in different works will indicate that you are becoming more knowledgeable *and* are recognising authorities.
- Check in the prefaces or forewords of books for mentions of your topic.
- Be aware of possible rival or alternative hypotheses or interpretations of data.

(b) Be selective.

- Only read information which is relevant to your topic. You may only need to read a particular section or part of a chapter from a book. Checking the contents page and the index of a book will help you here.
- Assess the importance of what you read. How reliable are the findings of any research? What is the relevance for your chosen topic?

If you are breaking new ground, then in your paper you will need to discuss the reasons for the lack of literature pertaining specifically to your topic area. What areas need to be researched? Are you able to extrapolate ideas from other research or literature to use in your topic area?

3. WRITING THE PAPER

You should produce a balanced, coherent piece of work which compares ideas from more than one source. Ensure that you provide additional comment on these ideas and do not merely present them. Be selective and, where appropriate, use source materials to support or challenge a particular position in your work.

Do not worry if, as you write, you deviate somewhat from your original outline. You may have discovered interesting information or developed lines of thought which you had not originally been able to anticipate.

4. WRITER'S BLOCK

The term *writer's block* is used to describe the condition in which your mind goes blank and you have no ideas, or you feel that you cannot express your ideas clearly. This strikes all writers at some time. It can be interpreted as a healthy sign that you are overtaxing the brain in one particular way and should not be a cause for alarm. The following hints may help:

(a) Read over what you have written.

(b) Try recopying sections of your work. You may find that ideas occur to you while you are doing this. Note the ideas down (even if they are one word only). Try extending the ideas into sentences.

(c) Relax and do something else. Later you may find that your mind has cleared.

(d) Move to a different section of your work and try working on it.

(e) Do something fairly mechanical, such as writing out your contents and bibliography page. You will have spent time productively and given your mind the opportunity to process your ideas.

(f) Proof-read your work (see Section 6 below).

(g) Go back to your reading sources, or read a related article or chapter. Reading frequently will improve your writing skills, suggest ideas and clarify your thoughts.

5. REVISING

Revising your work means checking for any improvements that need to be made. You may have to do this one or more times before you write your final draft.

(a) Organisation:
- Have you presented your work in the most effective way?
- Is there a logical presentation and progression of ideas or do paragraphs/ sections need re-ordering?

(b) Content:
- Is the content appropriate to the title and the introduction?
- Is there a clear presentation and development of ideas?
- Is all information relevant? Check for any information that may be interesting but is irrelevant to the topic, redundant or repetitive.
- Do you give reasons for the points you introduce?
- Do you incorporate too much or too little supporting information?

(c) Clarity:
- Is the reader able to follow your line of reasoning?
- Have you integrated important ideas/sources of information when and where required, and in a clear way?
- Do all sentences/paragraphs have a logical connection with preceding/ following sentences/paragraphs?

(d) Language:
- Have you selected an appropriate level of formality (e.g. no use of contractions such as *it's* instead of *it is*)?
- Is your language too complex or too simplistic?
- Is your linguistic referencing too vague (e.g. over-use of pronouns or imprecise vocabulary)?
- Have you kept to the objective structures that characterise academic writing, such as impersonal forms and passive verbs?

(e) Clear sections:
- Have you written a clear introduction and conclusion?

(f) Reference to sources:
- Have you acknowledged all sources and given clear bibliographical details?
- Have you integrated your material (including any tables and illustrations) clearly and at relevant points in your work?

6. PROOF-READING

Proof-reading means checking your work for errors in spelling and style and checking that you have met the format requirements of your subject/department.

(a) Features of language use that you should check include:
  • subject/verb agreement
  • verb tense
  • the presence of a verb in a sentence
  • the presence of a subject in a sentence
  • word order
  • correct word class (e.g. noun, adjective, adverb, verb)
  • punctuation
  • linking words to show logical progression of ideas.

(b) Layout
  See Unit 4.

7. LATIN ABBREVIATIONS AND WORDS COMMONLY USED IN ACADEMIC WRITING

The following Latin abbreviations and words are commonly used in academic writing. Several of them have been used in this book:

Abbreviation	Latin	English meaning
c. or ca	circa	approximately, about (for dates)
cf.	confer	compare
e.g.	exempli gratia	for example, for instance
et al.	et alii, et alia	and other people/things
etc.	et cetera	and so on, and the rest
et seq.	et sequens	and the following pages
ibid.	ibidem	in the same place (usually referring to a reference)
i.e.	id est	that is, in other words
inter alia	inter alia	among other things
loc. cit.	loco citato	in the place mentioned
NB	nota bene	note well or carefully (for an important point)
op. cit.	opere citato	in the work mentioned before
passim	passim	at many points, recurrent
viz.	videlicet	namely (naming someone/something you have just referred to)

Some of the above abbreviations may be new to you. Only use them in your own writing if you are confident you are using them correctly. Reading widely and noting when and how they are used will help you assess their correct use. Below are examples of how some of the abbreviations may be used.

(a) *et al.* This is used when a book was written by joint authors/editors. Only the first author/editor is given in your paper to save space. Refer to the bibliography for the names of the other authors/editors (e.g. Ochs *et al.*, 1983: 71).

(b) *ibid.* When making consecutive references to a particular source, *ibid.* can be used instead of repeating the name of the author and the book. If the page number is different from the one previously mentioned, this can be given after *ibid.* (e.g. *ibid.*, p. 22).

(c) *loc. cit.* This is used when references to a source are not consecutive but the later reference comes closely after the earlier one. It refers to the same author, book *and* page as the earlier reference.

(d) *op. cit.* This is used when references to the same source follow each other closely but are not consecutive. *Op. cit.* comes after the author's name, and is followed by a page number, i.e. it is like *loc. cit.* except that the page number is different.

Below are examples of references as they might occur in a text:

1. (James: 1991) – normal reference.
2. (Watkins: 1970: 93) – normal reference with page number.
3. (*ibid.*) – repeats reference 2.
4. (*ibid.*, p. 83) – repeats reference 2, but with a different page number.
5. (James, *loc. cit.*) – repeats reference 1.
6. (James, *op. cit.*, p. 57) – repeats reference 1, but with a different page number.

UNIT 5

WRITING THE EXTENDED ESSAY: TASKS

MAIN TASK

In this task you will produce a research paper of 2,000–3,000 words on a topic related to your area of study. The topic selected should be specific in nature. (You may decide to follow up in depth an aspect of the topic you selected for your essay in Unit 4.) You should expect to refer to at least five sources of information.

The greater specificity of the topic you select means that you have to be more selective when choosing source materials. You will probably find that no one article or book deals solely with your topic. In this case you may have to extract relevant information from a wide variety of sources and from source material which may not deal directly with your chosen topic.

Your topic should neither be too complex nor too simplistic. Refer to the 'Guide' section of this unit for how to select your topic and approach the writing phase. You should attempt to improve on any areas of weakness revealed in your Unit 4 essay.

ADDITIONAL TASK

In the course of this book, you have looked at legitimate ways of incorporating information from other sources and the conventions of presenting an acceptable piece of academic writing. In the following task, you will find examples of wrong language usage which is *not* grammatical or structural and which has not so far been dealt with in this material (except very briefly in Unit 3, Task 10). You may be able to identify some of these types of wrong usage in your own work. The task is not intended to provide you with an exhaustive checklist of non-grammatical errors. However, it might help you in the final stages of your work by drawing attention to some weaknesses you may be less aware of.

Read the extract below and then consider the pieces of writing that follow it. These deal in various ways with some of the content of the extract – some paraphrase its contents; others challenge the writer's point of view.

You are *not* intended to scrutinise the writing carefully for suitability or accuracy of *content*, as you have done with several previous tasks of this kind. Your task is to decide whether the pieces of writing that follow the extract would be acceptable as academic writing. If not, identify the fault as precisely as you can and discuss it with your teacher.

> As has been suggested above, the term 'Third World' may have outlived its usefulness. Its use may in fact serve to perpetuate the dependence of lower-income countries on imports from the industrialised world. Advanced technology may be incompatible with the internal realities of those countries, leading to disruptive effects on local lifestyles and the environment. For example, large-scale energy installations may make little sense in predominantly rural societies in which energy from the sun or wind can be harnessed relatively cheaply in the form of small, solar-powered devices or windpumps.

(From R. Grant, 'Future patterns', unpublished monograph, July 1992.)

Text 1

Let's face it, the term 'Third World' is now distinctly old hat. Even if there's little sign of the gap between the richest and poorest nations narrowing, the end of the Cold War some years ago makes the long-established classification less than useful. It's high time it was done away with, and the absence of any other all-embracing term that might be satisfactory only goes to show we'd be better off considering countries individually rather than lumping them all under one dubious category.

Text 2

Families uprooted from areas where their people have lived for generations, perhaps centuries, a way of life that is close to the land destroyed. The question we must ask ourselves is, is it worth it? Is it worth paying this price for the progress that advanced technology promises? Is it worth risking displacement and greater unhappiness for scores of people? Is it worth paying hard-earned money which would be better spent on more basic necessities? The answer, my friends, *must* be no!

Text 3

There is little reason to doubt that, taking into account the undoubtedly enormous costs that could be incurred in the adoption of large-scale projects, it would be advisable for many countries that lack sufficient funds to undertake the construction of large energy installations to consider resorting to other sources, on what is likely to be a substantially smaller scale. This might involve, for example, the harnessing of energy from the sun in the form of small, solar-powered devices or utilising windpumps, two options that may be feasible in a large number of cases, even taking into account the fact that the initial expenditure on such alternative projects may seem relatively high at this point in time.

Text 4

As a matter of fact, many countries cannot afford advanced technology. It can be said that a preferable course of action for such countries would be to resort to other forms of technology. The utilisation of small-scale energy installations rather than large ones is a case in point. It goes without saying that this is not always feasible. Indeed, a large nuclear power installation may in fact be considerably cheaper than the introduction of solar-powered devices or windpumps, contrary to what is sometimes maintained (see, for example, Grant, 1992).

Text 5

I think that for many countries in the so-called 'third world' it is extremely expensive to utilise advanced technology. It can lead to dependence on imports from the countries producing that technology, as well as upsetting local lifestyles and causing environmental damage. From my point of view, a sensible option is to adopt cheaper, small-scale alternatives. For example, I am inclined to think that introducing windpumps may, in some instances, be infinitely preferable to a large installation.

Text 6

The next point I should like to draw your attention to is a matter of considerable importance which has so far not been dealt with in this essay. I would like to raise the question of the suitability of advanced technology in the developing world. Critics have often commented on the cost and incompatibility of such technology in countries which have not reached the stage of industrialisation (Grant, 1992). What sense is there, for example, in spending vast sums of money on large-scale projects when a country can cheaply and easily resort to small-scale ones?

Text 7

As Grant (1992) suggests, it is absolute nonsense to expect a developing country to introduce large-scale energy plants when it can harness energy far more cheaply from the wind and the sun on a small scale. Only a completely naive simpleton could believe that an inevitable outcome of using one form of advanced technology would be to lead automatically to the development of other forms in the country concerned. It is patently obvious that when developing countries acquire advanced technology from the industrialised world it only serves to further the chronic dependence of the former on the latter.

Text 8

Last but not least, some attention must be given to the matter of suitability of technology. To adopt advanced technology or not to adopt it, that is the question. It is not in every case that small-scale alternatives prove to be cheaper. In fact, in the case of some types of technology, such options may be few and far between.

Text 9

Research by Grant (1992) established conclusively that advanced technology may often not suit poorer countries. As he discovered, in places where cheap utilisation of solar energy is possible, large-scale energy installations may not be the best option.